About the

Paul & Jan Allen have researched : to Crack the Morse Code' for the pa in working as a location scout/ data nurse.

This fascinating journey evolved from their love of the Inspector Morse T.V series, and careful nurturing led the couple from Oxford's town and gown to the wild windswept beyond.

To celebrate the twentieth anniversary of the first airing of the Inspector Morse series, which went out on the 6th January 1987, the book is unique in its view of the series.

The authors have met many of the cast, crew and public involved in the dramatisation of Colin Dexter's novels. This has led to a compilation of recollections and narrative accounts from the thirty-three Inspector Morse episodes and the new Lewis series.

By means of personal memories and antidotes, the individuals who worked on the series explain the roles of the cast and crew.

With new locations unearthed, the authors travelled to the scenes to reminisce with the characters who were involved in the filming, whether directly or indirectly.

Discover how a sixty plus film crew could descend on your house, how a pub becomes transformed back one hundred and forty years, or how a church adopts a gothic feel from the people who were there.

Whether you have an interest in the technological arena of filming, an affectionate recall of the Inspector Morse series, or a curiosity over the locations, the authors hope that the following journey will be as much of an adventure for you as it was them.

ENDEAVOURING
TO
CRACK
THE
MORSE
CODE

PAUL & JAN ALLEN

INTRODUCTION

In the mist of the dreamy spires of Oxford, the story unfolds and so the very essence of an Inspector Morse begins.

An Oxford trained scholar, yet cynical of the deep-seated traditions. Portrayed as a real ale and Glenfiddich drinker, an avid crossword solver, and a classical music lover, Inspector Morse pursues murderers in a Mark 2 Jag. The car is completely devoid of electronics and contemporary intervention.

Nevertheless, he remains heavily focused on chasing the sincere ethics of society, as he perceives them. His every step devotedly accompanied by his family loving, dependable, Geordie Sergeant-Robbie Lewis.

A novelist uses words to paint a picture. To create a programme that retains a place in television history, involves a team working together to produce a vision that lingers.

The Inspector Morse television series evolved from the inspirational characters of the novelist Colin Dexter. His extensive, talented imagination whilst on holiday in Wales led to a compilation of award winning detective books. The novel origins of Morse portray a pub crawling, prostitute searching Inspector with an older Sergeant accompanying him. The novel later caught the eye of the late television producer Kenny McBain. With great foresight and the ability to create an innovative screen drama, his team then adapted the characters to the memorable partnership that became so familiar on screen.

With intuitive casting of John Thaw for the role of the Inspector and Kevin Whately as his sergeant, the scene was set. Carlton waited with baited breath to see how the public responded - not only to the pristine characters, but also to a lengthy two-hour programe. The reaction was dramatic with viewing figures spiraling to nineteen million viewers at its pinnacle. Inspector Morse became one of the most successful detective series on British television, its global allure firmly establishing it as part of British and International television history.

For Inspector Morse to reach such an impressive accolade the enticing Colin Dexter's storylines fully absorbed the imagination. Together with Carlton's superb production management and casting, an additional quality is the captivating Oxford locations and traditions of the town and gown.

It is without doubt that the locations played an important part in the success and that Colin Dexter's love of Oxford inspired the original choice of the locations. Adapting this to the screen took four main location managers -Russell Lodge, Dennis Firmanger, Charles Hubbard, and Alan Pinniger, alongside Robert Raynor and Martin Lee. With Russell Lodge continuing to work on Harry Potter, Dennis Firmanger on Midsommer Murders, Alan Pinniger on the new Lewis series, the selection speaks for itself.

However, it is more than just finding an appealing spot that fits the storyline!

It is in the appreciation of the process of adapting a novel along its convoluted pathway to transmition that justifies the choice of a location. However, the use of assorted locations does initiate the viewer sometimes questioning the familiar. Is the unmistakably recognizable scene actually Oxford and not the familiar local sight as first believed? Does the initial unyielding impression that it is in Oxford continue to manifest sufficient doubt to defy any preceding certainty?

Was Inspector Morse filmed in Oxford?

MEET THE BOYS (AND GIRLS)

The principal creative driving force is the director, who works with the producer. The Producer's role is raising funds, hiring key personnel and arranging for distributors. He hires the heads of the teams and they in turn hire their team. The director communicates to the actors their vision of the final production. Generally, they have complete artistic control although in larger productions they may delegate smaller scenes to second units. A financial budget is agreed. Major expenses called above the line expenses are committed to before production. This includes story rights, salaries, travel, living, and production costs. Anything else is below the line expenses. An assistant director's duties include tracking the progress of filming versus the production schedule, a detailed plan of timings, preparing call- sheets which are a listing of which actors will be required for which scenes, and when they will be required.

The original novelist for Inspector Morse was Colin Dexter and Colin Dexter's books undoubtedly put the location for Inspector Morse in Oxfordshire. The books inspired the producers and they became transformed by the screen -writers into a screenplay. Julian Mitchell, a screen- writer for Inspector Morse describes how the series is heavily reliant on the written word, the 'words' carrying more weight than in most television programmes. Having the ideas is being halfway there. Once the book reaches the script department, the script editors will review the script and make changes based on the input from the directors and producers. A script supervisor then traces how the filming deviates from the script and ensures continuity. They produce a lined script where notes are kept corresponding to what has been filmed meaning the production team can see at a glance the scenes shot without having to look through reels of footage. The next step is to decide a planned shooting schedule. This is a detailed plan of the timing of activities associated with the making of a movie. This is decided between the producers, production manager, production co-coordinator, location manager, and director of photography (DOP) and all other heads of departments such as costume, make-up, sound, and lighting. Ideally, once a new series is decided, time would be sufficient to allow for full research.

The executive producer, producer and script- writer would meet to assign story lines. The executive producer would represent the people with the money and once the script is decided, he assumes control of the day-to-day running.

Waiting to meet Chris Burt in the affluent surroundings of the Morse Bar, at the Randolph Hotel, Oxford, the photographs of the filming of Inspector Morse and Lewis radiate a feeling of familiarity. Late, due to filming allows time for an appreciation of the atmosphere carefully created, but effortlessly portrayed by the courteous staff. The ambiance notably changes as he saunters towards the table. Simultaneously, as he sits down a Jameson and water has appeared silently in front of him. Obviously, a well liked and regular customer, welcoming greetings emerge from staff appearing through disclosed doorways. Similarly acknowledged, Lawrence Fox enters and almost as if to script, he becomes engrossed in mobile phones and laptops. Both men well mannered and affable, despite filming being in progress since eight that morning .The filming for the new Lewis series had been at The Mal Maison Hotel . The hotel being ideal for a script line of an ex con being released from prison and resuming his activities, then having accommodation provided in a hotel resembling a prison. With the Student's union close by, the day's locations were just a short walk away from the Randolph Hotel.

Chris Burt begins to explain why he felt Inspector Morse was so popular. High-quality writers, prominent actors throughout, classical music, Oxford- with the Gown and Town, and leading directors ensured it would be successful. Having joined the team in The Last Enemy, by then John Thaw was highly respected in the role of Morse. His acting retained the familiar brilliance, despite personal dilemmas. A simple look could cover a paragraph of script making it superfluous. Kevin's facial expressions could read chapters and an affinity with Lawrence Fox was evident. From the older generation portraying Morse immersed in policing as it was, pre occupied with the gown and grammar, Lewis provided the younger generation. As time moves on the genuinely technophobic Kevin Whately reminisces as he teams up with the technical loving Lawrence Fox. The pilot series of Lewis was the top programme for ITV amassing over eleven million viewers.

Similar to the attributes that made Morse so popular, Daniel Boyle remains the writer for Lewis and although much of the team had been changed to give the programme a new look. Alan Plater has also joined the team as a writer. Recently arriving in Oxford to begin a four -week filming, the locations started with the Ashmolean museum.

The filming was for three episodes and took part in the format of six days shifts followed by five day shifts, from eight am to nine pm. Chris O'Dell remained the DOP, Barrington for music and Alan Pinniger for location manger. Having attended Jesus College Chris Burt was familiar with the 'Gown'. Alan having attended Worcester College was familiar with the perception of the Gown, an important prerequisite for a location manager to work conceptually in both Morse and Lewis. Important in filming both Morse and Lewis, an appreciation and understanding of architecture was also necessary. Chris felt that the main quality for a location manager was an ability to approach people in a manner that 'got them on side'.

Savouring filming in Oxford again, Chris felt the buildings were a great attribute- although people still stopped to stare. Filming a large scene the previous night had meant some post editing to remove anyone looking at the camera. Perhaps this is could act as a gentle reminder that if passing filming and wishing to remain as part of the footage, do not look at the camera but at the 'event' that is being filmed! His favourite colleges for filming included Exeter for the large raised area to film down into the quads and the backdrop of the Radcliffe Camera and All Souls. Together with the gentle beauty of Magdalen, the gardens of Trinity, the old walls around New College and the archways of Merton College, it was a director's delight. Previously difficult to film at, St John's College would now be appearing in future episodes of Lewis.

With the cost of hotels and other expenses associated with shooting on location, Oxford as a location depicted the 'place'. Anything else would be studio or near the studio. For instance, an optician appearing in Lewis could be anywhere and did not need to be in Oxford, but the view from a particular optician's reception in Oxford showed recognizable Oxford buildings. The particular reception area so became a location in the new Lewis, the rest of the opticians elsewhere. As with many of the houses in Morse, the houses in Ealing represent the architecture of the Don's houses in Oxford. Hence, most of the Oxford Don's houses were in Ealing as it was nearer the studios. It is why much of the filming was in Hertfordshire or Surrey.

As in describing The Way through the Woods, a wood is just a wood and so it was closer and more convenient to film in Woods in Surrey. The only problem was that the woods chosen were near Gatwick Airport and so plane noise needed removing.

The favourite episode of Chris Burt's was 'The Wench is dead'. Traveling from Wales to the Midlands and down through to the Kennet & Avon Canal, the props, and concept produced stunning results. John Thaw had not been involved in any of the Victorian scenes and so did not see them until screened. Delighted with the results he was promptly on the phone to Chris to congratulate him. Another episode was 'Remorseful Day', with the enchantment of 'In Paradisium, it was also the first time John Thaw had ever played the part of a dying man. The scene filmed in the mortuary meant the crew themselves were in tears and the electrifying tensions and emotions remembered forever. In describing John Thaw's best role it was in Goodnight Mr. Toms (also produced by Chris Burt) and indeed it is also the role John Thaw described as his best.

As the talk lingered on to the people associated with Morse who had volunteered to participate in this book and discussions with people at the locations used that later appear in this book, it appeared that the memories were fond as the fascinating insight concluded with an order for several books on it's completion.

Once a script is prepared, a copy goes to the location manger. On receiving a script, he sets to work pinpointing possible locations.

Fundamentally, Oxford was key location for Inspector Morse and any filming at a place not constructed for production necessitates a location manger. The location manager liaises with the people at the locations and arranges with the authorities for permission to shoot in specific areas.

So what makes an ideal location and why is a location chosen?

A photograph means an image (or light) captured on paper. The art of capturing the picture is a little more complicated. For a start reference to what is a photographers 'eye'. A photographer will often 'look' at things differently and see a creative or artistic appeal. They will frequently 'see' the world in a different way and the art is to then record that image in the way they have perceived it. This may sound simple, but camera angles and an appealing subject is not enough! The angle although creative, needs composition to make it 'balanced'. The creativity and originality decided on, and then a depth of field needs to be included.

A depth of field is the measure of the range along a camera's line of site in which objects will be in focus, pertaining to aperture and shutter speed. This literally means that you travel into the shot and it draws your eye.

A favourite is often a bend in the road that can give a deep focus shot. A shot in which both the foreground and the background are in focus is a shot with exceptional depth of field.

Colour and tonal range means recording the shot with enough depth in the colour and tones to give a 3D effect. Technical appreciation is required as noise and grain to the picture can occur if there is not enough light or if the photographer cannot alter the settings to allow sufficient light. Lighting is all-important and can 'make or break' a shot. With that all in place then a dramatic effect, that tells a story in a glance makes the shot complete.

Of course though, if you are a location manager looking for that shot there are a few other things to consider!

The authority to film in the area, script dictating in an architectural and geographical sense, health and safety, physical logistics of filming, locality, and accessibility to studio, cast, and crew all play an important part in choosing the ideal location. Many of the filming and lighting units are from the Bristol area, so with distance and size of the vans needed, accessibility is essential.

Additional restraints may influence preferences, such as a church needs to be as adjacent to a house window or a shop needs to be next door to the murder scene. Then the perfect 'position' may not always allow parking facilities for the entire unit to be in place or for laying camera tracks, or lighting be sufficient.

Distance involved has to match the availability of the stars. Key equipment and personnel must be able to access the location at a precise time and day. Timing is all- important on location, locations cost money, so every minute has to work.

Other considerations concern where the filming is actually taking place. For illustration purpose, if the script requires a police station, an example of what is required would be-

Requests to film on police premises

➢ The PFD will deal with all initial location enquiries.
➢ Enquiries maybe via the related agencies

Individual Location Managers.

➢ PFD will identify the location and liaise with relevant areas and departments to ensure the necessary resources are available
➢ PFD will ensure all contracts are signed and invoices raised and confirmation supplied to the relevant area/dept.
➢ PFD will liaise with relevant departments and areas to establish a list of identified police premises, which may be suitable for filming.
➢ PFD will build a library of photos and information on suitable premises for filming with agreed charging rates.
➢ PFD will provide Corp Commission with outline story plans or scripts for approval prior to any agreement on filming.
➢ PFD would obtain the approval of Area Commander or Head of Department on the filming request.

➢ If there is agreement in principle then PFD will organize a meeting with the film company/agent and all other relevant members of the Constabulary to agree all the implications of the filming and to confirm the timetable of events, resources, and charges.
➢ The Constabulary must ensure the accompaniment of Film Company at all times when inside Constabulary locations.
➢ Area where filming is to take place should be checked for any police information which could be compromised e.g. on notice-boards, desks etc
➢ Advise must be given to surrounding staff filming is taking place, and any sensitive information, confidential offices/workstations should be locked away.
➢ If filming involves using a Constabulary computer careful consideration to screen content is essential e.g. crime system or database.

- ➢ Areas covered should include vetting, confidentiality and security, full details of the production, disruption factor, public perception, insurance, and liability and use of constabulary logo and other media issues.
- ➢ The company requesting filming or drama shall produce a site specific risk assessment and take into consideration the information provided by the PDF, on the Constabulary's risks and control measures.
- ➢ The PDF shall review the risk assessments from the filming company and ensure that any additional risks introduced by the combined tasks of the filming company and Constabulary, are risk assessed by both the PDF and the filming company.
- ➢ The PDF will ensure that the combined risk assessments, and any identified control measures to those members of staff, contractors, and members of the public and to anyone who maybe effected by the filming or drama.
- ➢ Documentation of the minutes of the meeting of what has been agreed and signed as agreed by all is required, as a formal record.
- ➢ The Director of Support Services would then sign by the filmmaker and, on behalf of the Constabulary, a license / contract.
- ➢ The PFD will then liaise with Area/Department to confirm the resources.
- ➢ Fees are between £500 and £1000 per day for filming in police premises. Charges for the use of the insignia are more difficult to decide. Individual negotiations will take between the PFD and the filmmaker taking into account the resources used.

Request for Traffic Management Assistance

- ➢ Direct all enquiries to the relevant TMU. The TMU will assess if a police presence is required from either an initial telephone conversation or, where there is doubt, a site visit.

- Written confirmation in the form of a fax, from the Film Company to the TMU will ensure both parties have agreed the policing requirement.
- If no police presence is required then generate a log of the activity.
- If police presence is required, the TMU's will complete request for filming form and send to PFD to invoice.
- TMU's will liaise with Logistics and try to resource the area. If resources are not available from the area, TMU's will pass to PFD who will liaise with Events & Logistics to try to resource from other Areas.
- Logistics will complete a contact form of the allocated officer/s and fax to PFD.
- PFD will inform the relevant TMU within 24 hours of the officer/s allocated or that there are no resources available.
- The officer will have the overtime-confirmed 2 days prior to any filming taking place. This is to take into account the unpredictability of the film industry (filming schedules/ weather)
- A minimum charge of five hours for each officer at the appropriate rate confirmed with Finance.
- A cancellation charge of five hours per officer charged if cancellation occurs within 8 days.
- Once the filming has taken place the PFD will, from the 220 or via the contact form, confirm the actual hour involved in the filming and requests the invoice accordingly less the £100 admin deposit.
- In accordance to Constabulary's Health and Safety Policy; The company requesting filming or drama shall produce a site specific risk assessment and take into consideration the information provided by the PDF, on the Constabulary's risks and control measures.
- The PDF shall review the risk assessments from the filming company and ensure that any additional risks introduced by the combined tasks of the filming company and the Constabulary, are risk assessed by both the PDF and the filming company.
- The PDF will ensure that the combined risk assessments and any identified control measures communicated to those members of staff, contractors, and members of the public or anyone affected by the filming or drama.

Insurance

> ➤ All film companies will prove their insurance cover. PFD will take a copy of their health and safety policy and see proof of employment liability
> ➤ The Constabulary's Health and Safety Officer will check policies.

With the locations pinpointed, budget meetings with the production team, property master, production designer, directors and location managers precede a "recce". A busload of crew visits each location, to gather the prerequisite information needed. Every location is first checked for suitability, what props would be needed, if there was room for tracks, camera angles, sound, lighting and electrical needs.

As a production designer on Inspector Morse, Robin Tarsnane would then ascertain the location's advantages.

He describes his role as -

"Entailing a scenario where on removing all the actors, everything else you see on screen would become my responsibility.

On receiving a copy of the script, locations are broken down into interior and exterior and together with the location manager suitable locations chosen. Some locations are not suitable inside, but the exterior is good quality. This means sending sketches and evaluations to a construction manager in order to first discuss proposals and then assemble some scenes in a studio elsewhere.

I can then confer characters with the director and art director or set director so that the initiation of sourcing props begins in order to authenticate the location. This involves detailed referencing, fabricating, and conception of the spirit and quintessence of each individual characterization.

Originally, sourced by verifying the occupation and assumed lifestyle necessary to depict a set that an actor keenly feels belongs to the character.

For instance if a prisoner is the character the actor is to feign, the stench of a prison cell, the threatening feeling of dread and trepidation are essential elements to creating the scene and are validated by authentic replication, utilizing vision, noise and aroma. Harmonizing with these impressions is the art department, preparing the lifelike, visual graphics. If a person picks up a paper in the Police Station, it has to be correct, with the suitable Thames Valley logo.

Exclusively published newspaper reproductions that complement scripts often demanding the composition of sheets of undetected transcripts, but has to be exact as backup should the camera settle on the script. Often this juncture resembles a forger's paradise.

In addition to identifying and researching these incidental background props, cars also need pinpointing, including ones for crashing- at which point the stunt director becomes involved.

Consideration is given at this point, as to whether blustery, wet, or wintry weather conditions are called for or for instance, if bleak snowfall or turbulent wind is obligatory for the scene. Explosions, torrential floods or blazing fires may be an acknowledged as prerequisite during this time and need more intense fore planning.

Alternatively, a period drama or detective series may entail weapons or stagecoaches where official requirements need meeting. With this in progress, often once establishing a location as available, an actor is not, so necessitating supporting location.

Additional concerns such as noise levels, the disruption to the area and the availability of such practicalities as accommodation and food need addressing. For instance, scenes at a pub would mean that the props manager would ascertain if the pub glasses are accessible or if non- alcoholic beer would be available. Filming at the universities would necessitate checking such details as if there is the availability for three rooms close to each other, one to film in and two for storage, plus the logistics of getting the props up the narrow winding staircases to the scene".

With the first demands of the catering team for water identified, rubbish removal and the proprietor's needs are established. Make up teams would then decide on an area for make-up. For example, at the Trout in Oxford, this was often an area inside the pub itself. Timing of the filming was of course important. To take over a busy pub would be expensive, so would mean filming out of pub hours for short scenes. The universities are more available in holiday times.

The property master is the person responsible for buying, acquiring, and/or manufacturing any props needed for a production. The property master is also responsible for all aspects of prop use on the set and, in conjunction with the script supervisor, for maintaining set continuity.

Sound is an important factor. In one episode, the locations for an Oxford cloister changed to Eton. Each time an airplane went over, filming stopped. Airplanes do not fly at that altitude over Oxford!

The sound crew involves a sound designer, sound editor, sound effects, sound mixer, sound recordist, boom operator, re-recording mixer, music supervisor, and Foley artist. The sound designer creates the audio component of a movie, with the sound editor editing the soundtrack.

The Sound Effects Editor would then specialize in editing the sound effects in the post -production stage. The sound mixer who works with a boom operator completes the process of recording sound during production. As described by Steve Fish, the boom operator on set with Lewis, there are several significant factors to this.

"The technical sound aspects mean the whilst there are some very sophisticated tools available to the post production sound team, generally there isn't the time or resources available to do much with extraneous noises. The rule of thumb is if you can hear it on the set, you will hear it on the track!

Continuity problems with aircraft or other superfluous noises on some shots in a scene are often resolved by adding more planes to the other shots, creating the impression that the plane flies over throughout the scene (not an option on period drama of course). Often the simplest remedy is to do the shot again after the plane has gone.

Boom microphones are usually the first choice as they capture not only the best quality sound but can also give a much more natural "perspective". Personal microphones are a useful tool for situations where use of a boom is impossible. Often due to logistics of location or shot and in some circumstances their inherent insensitivity means they can perform well in extremely noisy locations (traffic, machinery etc).

However, points to remember:-

1) Clothing noise is very difficult to reduce.

2) You do not normally listen to someone's voice by pressing your head to their chest!

3) It is extremely difficult to create an illusion of perspective i.e. depth."

Barrington Pheloug composed or selected the music. Every piece heard or composed well- thought out and meaningful. Bearing in mind that the location also has to lend itself to the music and vice versa and this becomes an important part of the equation.

(Picture kindly provided by Barrington)

The Director of Photography (DOP) is ultimately responsible for the process of recording a scene in the manner desired by the director.

The Director of Photography has a number of possible duties such as selection of film stock, cameras, and lenses; designing and selecting lighting, directing the gaffer's placement of lighting; shot composition (in consultation with the director); film developing and film printing. Also called a_cinematographer, they are a person with great expertise in the art of capturing images either electronically or on film. This is through the application of visual recording devices and a selection and arrangement of lighting.

The role of the cinematographer's concerns the conceptual aspect of the filming, discussing and planning the approach to filming with the director. During this time, they analyze the script, story structure, characters, and visual approach. They discuss the concept with the production designer and ascertain budgets.

Once decided, the team then recce the place with the location manager, check sun positions and times, local weather, approve props, visit rental houses, and familiarize themselves with any new equipment. The next stage on the recce is to decide on design and lighting fixtures and discusses this with the gaffer and key grip.

The cinematographer will then follow the construction of the set through, approving lighting, walking the set with all departments to discuss requirements. Approve colours and textures, working with the assistant director to organize a shooting schedule and supervising the lighting crew. The technicalities of buying film, organizing shooting manpower, and getting the equipment, whilst maintaining contact with the other heads of department all fall under his responsibility. The staff using the new hired or bought equipment try the apparatus before vendors are paid, all unused parts returned at the end of the day. Testing and rehearsals allow any necessary changes to ensure the best advantage of portraying the visual aspect of the storyline, projecting the style and dramatic effect to ensure the best capturing of the mood. It also allows for consultation with other departments, such as sound or stunts. As shooting begins, a camera log- book notes all movements before the projected rushes are viewed with the director, producer, editor and camera crew. Whilst in production, teaching of new actors mean movie techniques are learnt, such as hitting marks etc and a ladder effect of training ensures staff continually learn and move upwards. The shots would now be graded, quality controlled and shown to the director for final approval. The technical formatting prepares the film, with publicity shots circulated the cinematographer then needs to be available for any archiving, reprint or transfer to different film media.

Clive Tickner was the cinematographer on some of the original Inspector Morse episodes. He describes the first episode of Morse as particularly great.

"John Thaw was very keen, it was a new and different project for him, and he put his all into it. The show was very highly funded for TV at that time, possibly around £800.000 an hour, at least £300,000 more than other shows at the time making it was very high profile. This meant good equipment, cranes, tracking vehicles and all the stuff of a decent feature film.

The job briefly involves getting on with director, understanding and discussing his ideas then putting them into practice. Light scenes to be interesting, to express the mood of that part of the plot, to use lenses to involve or to distance the audience according to plot needs. I need to get on with the artists, often expanding on the notes given them by the director. It entails being conversant with the budget and ordering equipment within that financial plan. Asking additional crew when needed within the budget and shoot at such a speed as to maintain quality but not hold up the schedule. The aim is to give a 'look' to the single show and to the series as a whole. To make interiors and exteriors appear to match plus to have the same 'look' as the whole. It goes on

"I was keen at the time on shooting movies on Panavision. Coincidentally Panavision brought out a 16mm camera at that time- so we shot the show on that. The camera had all the advantages of the 35mm equivalent, great 4-pin registration, good video take off, lots of quality lenses, etc., etc. The camera name came from after 'Elaine' the President of Panavision's wife. Peter Hammond is a very interesting director for a DOP. His first notes were-do not put the light where people expect it. Light a character's body maybe, or the background, or some other detail in frame, but not the obvious; i.e.; the face.

He also liked to break up the frame, shooting through various real or contrived foreground pieces, a fad that continued with later directors too. Kenny McBain, the very enlightened producer wanted a good new look for the show and backed us up on anything quirky we wanted to do. Peter was also always good for a joke or comment to keep the enthusiasm of cast and crew going.

We laughed a lot throughout the series. Choosing a favourite director would have to be Alastair Reid, great to be with. Later working with him on "Traffic" lead to a BAFTA, the first personal award I received. Alastair was big on tracking, we always took extra rails when working with him as he often worked out a whole scene in one shot, which required some neat moves to 'mop up'. Sometimes he would compose the action to fit into one long lens shot. A very imaginative man and a lovely person to work with, at the end of his first show, he tore up the last page of the script, much to Kenny's amazement and annoyance.

Alastair said with the story told, the end, as written, was unnecessary rubbish. He was right, of course. I know Kenny got a bigger audience than expected, but John Thaw certainly thought the show was going somewhere and to my knowledge those early shows have been aired around five times in this country alone, so all in all, the shows made a lot of money.

I think John Thaw did not want to keep pressing on, but needed a breather. It was very full on for him, he was in every shot, practically. Had a lot to learn and had to dash around and also, I think that working scripts had only been written for the first three episodes, as they didn't know how successful the show would be. The filming took the format of seasons; the first break allowed the scriptwriters a reasonable time to adapt the next set of stories. A two- hour show takes some writing.

In some later episodes, we struggled to find a place for an exterior to remind the audience where the plot was set. The first episode had to locate the people, the environment, the infrastructure etc. Possibly this was the reason for choosing 'In the Dead of Jericho' first.

Kevin was always a 'gent', accepting in the stories that he was subservient to Morse. He was good fun, took notes from both directors and John Thaw with equanimity. He put a great deal into his character and made a great foil for Morse. John put a lot into his character too, expanding the grumpy old boozer from the original. They were both great for the crew. They knew their names, always said 'Good morning'. Does not sound much, but when you shoot a whole picture and the stars do not even know your name by the wrap party, well, it was noticeable. They were also great for the new actors coming on, whether walk- on actors or bigger parts- they made them all feel welcome to the show, and helped them when the new guys were unfamiliar with the nuances of the scripts or production itself.

Russell Lodge was obviously very good, he found us excellent locations. Often we could not shoot the interiors of places we were using as exteriors but he always found us a good match elsewhere. This was often the case when shooting in Oxford. The budget only allowed for a few days there, so he would have to find, in and around London, interiors to match the Oxford buildings.

My worse memory was shooting on a church roof in 'Service of all the Dead'. It was very high, no walls and scary. Another dodgy memory was a shoot that finished late, with the camera crew worn out. We went for a drink (and snack) in a club near Westbourne Grove and got to chatting. After a while, we looked out and could not understand why it was not dark yet, we thought we had wrapped at dusk. We had talked all night and it was now morning. Somewhat worse, for wear, we still got to the location! A liberal helping of oxygen meaning we were able to get through the day! Generally, it was a great show, great crew, all my friends, and terrific cast and directors. I learnt a lot.

I do remember one particular scene from 'In the Dead of Jericho' where there is a village green, a post box, a bike, and a phone box. All the props were ours as they were required in the scene. Whilst we were filming a man, who, if he lived around there, must have known that normally there was not a phone or post box on the green, came up, and posted a letter. Later we discovered that he had posted his Pools coupon- so, later, we put it in a regular box, not wanting him to miss a possible win on the football results.

When arriving to shoot at Richard's office in 'The Dead of Jericho' the secretary had dealt with all the arrangements, but apparently, the boss did not know anything about it and was not happy! So everything did not always go according to plan"

Casting is the process of hiring the actors for the characters within the script and is typically the role of the casting director with input from the directors, producers, or studios.

Continuity comes under scrutiny and relates to the degree a movie is consistent. During filming a continuity check- list records the events during filming. This includes production and crew identification, camera settings, environmental conditions, the status of each take, and exact details of the action that occurs. Continual photographs of the filming and detailed notes kept.

The dialogue editor assembles, synchronizes, and edits all the dialogue in a film or television production. Usually they will use the production tracks, the sound recorded on the set. If any of the production tracks are unusable they can be replaced by either alternate production tracks recorded on set or by ADR, automated dialogue replacement, which is recorded after the shoot with the actors watching their performances in a sound studio and rerecording the lines. Once the dialogue editor has completed the dialogue track, the re-recording mixer then mixes it with the music and sound effects tracks to produce the final soundtrack.

Harry Barnes worked on Inspector Morse as the dialogue editor. His role was to clean up the original dialogue by taking out off screen noises and filtering superfluous sounds. Making clearer alternative takes if necessary. He would then go through this with the director and discuss which scenes need replacing due to background noise, performance, or new lines for plot reasons. This is then mixed in with the original and if well done are hopefully never noticed! Dialogues on this took two days to mix and two days to add effects, before showing the final mix to the director. This is then shown to the executives and notes and updates are then added.

Other members of the team include the costume designer who designs the costumes. A costume supervisor being the person in charge of costumes, usually preparing them for use and making sure they are accurate and faithful to the designs. Other responsibilities include consulting with the designers and training, supervising, and scheduling the costume staff. The costumes have to be decided and a log kept for continuity. Scenes are not shot in sequence and so it has to be recorded whether a shirt was undone, a tie done up.

The Makeup Supervisor is responsible for decorations placed directly on the skin or hair of an actor for cosmetic or artistic effect, with practitioners called artists.

It is only on ascertaining that the entire dynamics are correct that creates an ideal 'spot'. Once these details are in place groundwork can begin.

With everything in pace, call sheets are devised to log every movement, location, catering needs, weather forecasts, car movements, cast, and crew. Updated daily these are now available to cast and crew online. Planning each day geographically allows for the logistics and budgeting of filming. Overnight stays create hotel bills; excessive travel fuel and car hire costs.

The creation of transport movement orders document every detail, providing the information for cars used to ferry actors and crew. These will often later double as cars used on set. Parking and the movement of parked vehicles is continuous to ensure proximity as is necessary. With a team of eighty or more, the vehicles necessitate some order to allow proximity and freedom of movement. The movement orders also give directions and hotel accommodation details. They also document details such as refuse collection, security, and little reminders such as to wear blue over shoes when filming in the mortuary. They also include details of emergency services in the area. It is a strange territory to those working there. The location manager arranges all this. Most of the cars used at the later part of the Inspector Morse series were from Action Cars, based at Pinewood Studios.

A camera operator is a person that operates a film camera or video camera for the purpose of recording motion to film, video, or a computer storage medium. The operator is responsible not only for physically operating the camera, but for composition as well. The camera operator may collaborate with the actors and film crew to make technical decisions.

Andrew Speller worked 'Last seen Wearing' and he describes his role as follows:-

"A camera operator - on any shoot at its most basic does what it says on the tin. He operates the camera - that is he frames the shots, operates the moves, tells the grip where to lay tracks, gives the focus puller a very clear idea of the move/ the shot so that he can measure up distances and keep the image sharp. He then generally runs overseas the running of the camera crew behind the camera - (Focus, Loader, Grip) - but that is very much nuts and bolts description.

In the hierarchy of film, the Camera operator occupies the space between the Director and Director of Photography. You are serving two masters - it can be great or uncomfortable dependant on whether you form   a
creative working relationship with both of them. At its best it is THE BEST JOB ON THE CREW - Many DOP's now operate themselves, especially on TV drama (16mm) and less frequently, but still often, on features.

The reason being that you cannot beat looking through the camera to judge lighting, performance, composition and feel of a scene/take/shot - so it is the one job where all the creative elements of making images combine.

At its best, this trio of people works in harmony refining the effort of translating a script into moving images. The best Directors have a very clear vision as to how they want the film to look .They then share this with the DoP and Operator. Frequently the Operator /Director relationship on set is closer than that of Director / DoP .So on top of all the creative and technical skills the Operator needs to be a diplomat - orchestrating the ties between Director and DoP.

The other aspect is that the actors will often ask the operator how a take 'Felt' was it good for camera - was it good on them if they were pleased with it- the operator has to develop really good relationships with actors to build their confidence in their performances and in the operator's judgment.

Finally there is a good deal of skill - hand to eye co-ordination whether using fluid or geared heads - you need to know what equipment is best to achieve shots and it certainly helps to know what other people's jobs on your team involve. If you've come up through the camera department then that goes without saying - but sometimes when time pressure is on you need to make space for the focus puller or yourself and get a rehearsal - nobody says 'thanks' at rushes if the shot is soft (out of focus) or the move is executed badly. A good grip that is pushing the camera and operator about on the dolly is essential to help in reading the shot, following where actors go.

Some actors like to have exact positions to hit - others like to roam free - so its not all nailed down and exact and that is where teamwork really matters - Operator, Grip, Focus - inches out and its all go again". Experience does count on the floor so that adjustments made are   without any fuss, the actor does their 'thing' and the technical crew goes with it. It's all fascinating and I could go on but that's a fair start"

Josef de Baché-Kane, working on post- production in Morse and Lewis, describes how the specialty of Morse was excellent scripts, superb acting, and beautiful locations. Each episode was the individual director's creative vision. Morse always had great pacing, and superb camera work was married to excellent scripts. On set, the first Assistant Director ran the schedule of shooting scenes with the director, assisted by the second Assistant who made sure all the actors call sheets, costumes, make-up, and set props are in place and that everyone arrived as previously organized.

The second assistant often had a third Assistant who managed catering and transport for the set, further assisting in the needs of the director and actors on set. The filming created the essential sentiment of the team. Becoming closely knit the atmosphere of "family" grew around the series.

The post -production period follows a days filming schedule and after the principal photography is finished. The removal of the film or tape rushes from the camera results in "dailies" being produced on cassette copies made for the director, editor, and producers to view performance or perhaps re-shoot.

Once approved, the editor (working term "off-line"), determines with the director the best performances.

He weaves the storyline adding time for any effects required, for example, transitions between scenes. He works on a "rough-cut" as the crew will still be shooting and when principal photography is complete, he and the director will be in that darkened den of creativity that is the edit suite and so the post-production begins.

The assistant editor will have been digitizing all the rushes into an Avid or Lightworks editing system, naming each scene and takes and managing the bins they go into along with the administrative paperwork.

Simultaneously, the sound mixer will be re-recording any ADR (additional dialogue or any dialogue not clear on the shoot day) required and working with the composer for the music, he does this from cassettes produced from the editor.

The director and increasingly producers, working with the editor produce a "fine cut", when approved it is "locked" meaning no changes should be made as this affects negative cutters and sound mixers working simultaneously on the production.

The negative cutter cuts the film at his lab from the edit list, and a print forwarded to the telecine colourist, who sits with the director and DOP to enhance the look and feel of the production visually.

The next step is editing working term "on-line" editing and the sound layback processes. The on-line editor and sound layback mixer will usually be a different person from the editors. They complete the final process of 'conforming' the programe to the EDL edit list, the graphic designer or assistant editor creates opening and closing titles and any lower third captions, commercial breaks.

'Bumper stings' are inserted, and then you have a complete programe for transmission, in Morse's case on ITV, with exact timings for a one-hour slot in the schedule.

For the technically minded, the traditional post-production workflow film or videotape would be:

The Production.
Film or Videotape.
Film Laboratory or Create Editing Work Tapes
Editor Accesses Dailies via Cassettes, or Server etc.
Telecine Film Grade.
Director and Editor make final edit decisions.
Picture Lock to EDL list.
Negative Cut to EDL list.
Dialogue mixed Sound and Music layback.
Digital fixes, effects, depot (film sparkle) correction and any other manipulations.
On-line assemble Editing and Titling.
Create Multiple Versions for delivery worldwide in different aspect ratios.

- generally UK delivery is 16:9 widescreen (but with titles in a 4:3 viewing title box to accommodate old style square TV sets, US delivery is 4:3 Full Frame picture but also high definition if shot in that format, this is future proofing your series.

Endeavoring to cipher the code spans much further afield as fresh stories and twists emerge. Yet, the enigma continues to question whether this is solely another detective story, just one more Oxfordshire anecdote or possibly a more complex fantasy?

Certainly, on researching a common comment from the councils and authorities in the locations used for Inspector Morse, was a somewhat tiresome retort of-

'Morse was filmed Oxford'.

In one particular antidote during research, the filming department of a council replied in such a manner. On asking specific questions about seven locations used, they further responded by e-mail in capital, bold lettering stating categorically that their county was not in any of the Inspector Morse episode. Filming was in Oxfordshire only.

Subsequent to this, many other locations appeared in the vicinity. Such then, is the potential power of suggestion through television and the remarkable talent of the location manager!

So, with everything arranged to the last detail, filming can begin and everything fall into place – or does it?

IN THE DEAD OF JERICHO

Aired on the 6th January 1987

Executive Producer Ted Childs

Producer Kenny McBain

Directed by Alastair Reid

Writer Anthony Minghella

Production Designer David McHenry

Location Manager Russell Lodge

Writer – Novel Colin Dexter

1.

The opening scene of the Cantorum choir harmonizing to the slower chords of My Soul there is a Country by C. Hubert Parry produces a relaxed atmosphere in pleasing surroundings. The setting surges with emotion in what was to become an established and admired series.

Remarkably akin to the fiery upbeat tempo of an episode from the Sweeny, the storyline blazes into action as Morse arrives at a garage in Southall (now a supermarket). Engineless and pushed into conflict, the polished gleam of the Mark Two Jaguar screeches to a standstill, Vivaldi's Gloria playing at full volume. It is a Saturday morning and Morse stumbles on a gang of fleeing thieves. Handcuffing one to his car soon results in a costly collision, as the gleaming jaguar seemingly purrs into the path of an escaping vehicle.

The surroundings change and under the appealing ceiling's artwork at The Royal Holloway Sanatorium, Virginia Waters, Surrey, it would certainly appear to be luxurious. Now transformed into private flats, the beautiful internal artwork is still evident.

The Royal Holloway Sanatorium, Virginia Waters, Surrey, was the legacy of Thomas Holloway. A self-made multi- millionaire who made his fortune in patent medicine paid the equivalent, today, of six million pounds for the painting in the sanatorium. The architect was William Henry Crossland who was greatly inspired by the early 16th Century Chateau of Chambord in the Loire Valley. The Sanatorium centres around two very large quadrangles, with a contrasting white Portland stone and red brick facade. It became a College for Women in 1879 before becoming private flats.

In fact filmed years before transmition, the choir sang the one harmony seventy five times surrounded by the derelict building. The reality of filming was of leaking ceilings, dilapidated corridors, declining rooms and with no audience.

A completely different scene greets the viewers on airing. Preparation and alteration transformed the area to represent not only the magnificent performance, but also affluent surroundings. The superb acoustics and lighting justified the reformation. The first episode soon started what was to become a trend of repetitive opening remarks during most interviews of an enthusiastic account of the excellent hospitality, friendly people, and mouthwatering food for all involved.

Now fully imprinted on the British television screen and in the minds of the British public, Morse had made its mark.

Delayed by the events of the morning, Morse belatedly merges with the choir for the final two bars. Uneasily, he smiles at the laughter.

As Morse and Anne Staveley journey back to the house in Canal Reach, they initially stop for a drink at the White Horse Inn, Broad Street, Oxford.

The surrounding architecture provides a dramatic backdrop and an insight into the town of Oxford. It introduces the audience to the history and landmarks that is Oxford. Historically, seemed to have little importance during the Roman Times and it was not until the Saxon period that Oxford began to give the impression of being important. A Saxon abbey was established where Christ Church now stands, and the abbess was St. Frideswide, a Mercian princess. The abbey later became Christ Church Cathedral.

It is in the Saxon period that Oxford begins to assume an importance missing from its Roman past. A Saxon abbey was established where Christ Church now stands, and the abbess was St. Frideswide, a Mercian princess.

Supposedly, St. Frideswide built the abbey as a means to preserve her virginity. A persistent suitor tried to take the abbey by force. Blinded by his effort until Frideswide restored the man's sight, Frideswide then became the patron saint of Oxford. St. Frideswide's abbey burnt to the ground in 1002, later rebuilt as an Augustinian priory.

During the late Saxon period, Oxford owed its growth by being on a major trade route between Mercia and Wessex, powerful Saxon empires.

Alfred the Great led the Saxon resistance against the Vikings. Alfred's interest in schooling led to claims that he funded the original Oxford Colleges. Coins found dating to this period also suggest there may have been a Royal Mint in Oxford.

As confrontation continued between the Saxon's and the Viking's, so the original defensive towers appeared. In 1071, the Norman Lord Robert D'Oily built Oxford Castle.

The growing importance of the town led to the establishment of many religious houses and churches in the town and surrounding area. Religion and learning were synonymous. This growth attracted teachers from Europe who set up in business by renting or buying houses and rooms and providing basic accommodation, food, and tuition to students forming the first academic halls. As there were no universities in England, Englishmen went to Europe, usually Paris, for a university education. This tradition came to an abrupt halt in 1167 with the expulsion of English students from Paris. Oxford, with its established culture of teaching and learning became the focus for continuing studying and the church of St Mary the Virgin became the focal point of the emerging university. Teaching expanded rapidly and at one stage, there were one hundred and twenty academic halls in the town centre alone.

Sometime in the late 11th or early 12th century, Oxford became a centre of learning for training clerics and by the 13th century, Oxford was in the center of European academia.

During the 13th century, wealthy benefactors established graduate colleges, with endowments of land and property to provide an income covering running costs. This enabled teaching students without charge and when this practice extended to undergraduate colleges with the foundation of New College in 1379, the future of academic halls was bleak; by the mid 15th century only eight remained.

Despite Oxford's growth in the medieval period, misfortune arose when a fire in 1138 burned the city to the ground. Later hit by the Black plague in 1348 -1350, the population of the city dropped dramatically and the colleges took full advantage of the situation by buying vacant property.

The change saw a rapid rise in the student population causing difficulties for the townspeople and the town / gown relationships became fraught. There were many riots over the years (including one in 1209 which resulted in a group of students fleeing Oxford and creating Cambridge University), but the most serious was in 1355 when a three day riot left sixty three students, and probably half that number of townspeople dead.

With stilted attempts at social interaction and vocal admiration, the voyage continues. Walking through the Old School Quads, they pass the prominent gargoyles at the Sheldonian.

Sir Christopher Wren built and designed the Sheldonian Theatre in 1664 -8, with funds donated by Gilbert Sheldon. Gilbert Sheldon during his long career held office as Warden of All Souls Bishop of London and Archbishop of Canterbury, later elected as Chancellor of the University of Oxford.

As the episode unfolds, the camera immediately pans to a recognizable landscape that firmly establishes the key location as Oxford. This practice becomes synonymous as a means of providing opening doorways to numerous future episodes. Irrespective of the actual locality, the initial impression suggests that the entire filming is in Oxford.

At this point, the eminent dreamy spires of Oxford appear as the camera pans the skyline.

The journey continues past the well- known Hertford Bridge as they leave the School Quad and enter Catte Street and on into the Radcliffe Square.

Oxford is the oldest university in the English-speaking world, it has thirty-nine official Colleges, and lays claim to nine centuries of continuous existence.

Hertford College lays claim to being one of the oldest Oxford Colleges. Originally established in the late 13th century, much of the current architecture added in the late 19th and early 20th centuries The College is over three small quads, Old, New, and Holywell. Unusually, a street separates the Old and New Quads. A pedestrian bridge, one of the most famous sites of Oxford, joins the quads. Hertford Bridge spans New College Lane in a short arc.

Sir Thomas Jackson built and designed much of the current architecture of Hertford College and the bridge.

Walking towards Brasenose College, Morse and Anne pass the Radcliffe Camera.

Brasenose Hall began transformation into Brasenose College in 1509. Built from stone from Headington Quarry, the founders of Brasenose College were Sir Richard Sutton, a lawyer, and William Smyth, Bishop of Lincoln. The Radcliffe Camera originated from £40,000 bequeathed by Dr John Radcliffe, the royal physician in 1737-1749. Today the Camera functions as the main reading room of the Bodleian Library. The finished building holds some 600,000 books in underground rooms beneath Radcliffe Square.

The camera then pans to the Radcliffe Observatory as Morse and Anne walk past The Bookbinders Arms and into Canal Reach.

Green College spreads over three acres of ground, dominating the College is the eighteenth-century Radcliffe Observatory. The building functioned as an observatory for 160 years from 1773 until 1934, when the previous owners (the Radcliffe Trustees) decided to sell it. The new purchaser in 1934 was Lord Nuffield who presented it to the hospital authorities. In turn, 1936 saw it established as the Nuffield Institute for Medical Research there. In 1979, the Institute moved to new premises in the grounds of the John Radcliffe Hospital, thus freeing the Observatory site for its new owner. Built with funds from the trustees of Dr. John Radcliffe whose considerable estate had already financed a new quadrangle for his old College (University College, Oxford) as well as the Radcliffe Library (now the Radcliffe Camera) and the Radcliffe Infirmary (1770) Building began in 1772 to plans by the architect Henry Keene, but only the Observer's House is his design. Keene's death in 1776 meant James Wyatt completed the Observatory to a different design.

The scene is set within a matter of minutes and remains so by such unquestionable techniques throughout the series.

The leisurely walk to the homes of both Anne Stavely and Jackson passes the Bookbinders Arms, concluding in the Oxford area of Jericho. Jericho is a stones throw from Oxford city centre, a small cosmopolitan area that is alive with restaurants, shops, and housing. The authenticity of Jericho is accurate, although the road name changes from Coombe Road to Canal Reach.

These scenes in Jericho provide a suitable juncture to sample the artistic creation of the production designer and props department in relation to character portrayal. The script suggests the need for two similar houses occupied by people with very different lifestyles and a distinct theatrical contribution creates the ideal residences.

Anne's home necessitates the more opulent dwelling befitting a classical piano teacher.

The relaxing green walls reflect tranquility with mirrors, plants, and pine. A grand piano and carefully chosen ornaments grace the front room. Further pine furniture and patchwork adorn the bedroom. The staircase remains uncarpeted; the slightest hint a home lovingly in the making.

Comparatively, Jackson's home pertains to an elderly, abandoned, and self-sufficient odd job man. Enterprising changes to the environment show bare light bulbs hanging forlornly from the peeling ceilings. Badly put together flat pack furniture and disorderly, chaotic belongings lay strewn haphazardly throughout the rooms. Rabbits monopolize the garden area and his enthusiast hobby is evident as the stench of stale fish invades the kitchen, the gutted remains proudly displayed on age-old newspaper wrappings.

With the role of Jackson, admirably played by the late Patrick Troughton, formerly the second Dr. Who, the full effect is completed.

Nestling amongst the cosmopolitan community the acquisition of the houses in Coombe Road, as a film set, is ideal.

The location was a quiet cul – de sac area with ample parking nearby. Houses opposite each other allowed a nosey neighbour to work as a voyeur and blackmailer. It later allows him the ability to incriminate Morse in the proceedings. It provided the ideal position to watch Morse's interest in Anne develop (perhaps even the first screen kiss for Morse) and monitor his increasing visits.

Jackson's home allowed for increasing intimate knowledge of Anne and all her other visitors. Jackson continued to watch with regular enthusiasm as Ned and Mr. and Mrs. Richards called. He also noted the initial meeting of Morse and Lewis, the promotion of Bell bringing Morse and Lewis together as a team.

The area is also renowned for difficulties in parking, a prominent part of the plot.

With Anne's suicide, Jackson was able to observe the police investigation first hand, although his interest in an address of Anne's lover suggests he had recently been in closer contact with Anne. Together with Morse's recollection of the fishy smelling phone box, Jackson's movements for the time of death could perhaps also be debatable.

The untimely, voyeuristic enthusiasm unfortunately waning as an interest in dubious literature meant he was gravely unaware of the impending visit from Mr. Richard's brother.

College Cruisers territory completing the requirements of a secluded area for Morse to navigate the back wall entering Anne Stavely's property undetected, apart from the unexpected appearance of Lewis spoiling his plans.

Many of the residents from the time of filming still remain. Newspaper articles record the events at the time. Filmed in the scorching heat of a 1985 summer's day it initiates a feeling of comradeship amongst those that know where the filming was. Exchanged fleeting, knowing glances pass between friends as Morse drives up one street, only to be several miles away within minutes. The hopeful recognition of a passing glimpse of someone you know keeps an avid watcher as the celebrated portrayal of both the town and gown unfolds. Many other Oxford residents later provided their homes for filming, but for this episode, the hustle and bustle of equipment and crew saturated the streets of Jericho.

The excitement as the filming commenced was seeing both Patrick Troughton and John Thaw. Local children were in awe, as the phenomenon of star spotting became the order of the day. The Bookbinders Arms became the central point for the congregating of cast and crew and the means for lighting the streets shining from the windows. A fire engine was in situ for the day, later spraying cool water over excited children. The crowd from just outside the Bookbinders watched the police siege, delighted, as many images of them watching were included in the final footage.

Another tradition began with the mismatching of fact and fiction. The residents of Coombe Road found that people believed they lived in the street where both a murder and a suicide took place. Following filming, the landlord of the Bookbinders Arms apparently received many enquiries, including one about rebinding a bible! Finally, a husband accused Colin Dexter of having an affair with his wife when he felt the character portrayal was a little too close to the truth.

Later recollections from Jackson because of an interrogation by Lewis reveal Morse's visits. An entangled Morse is implicated as more the murderer than detective. Lewis hurriedly researches the key issues at Gills & Co in Wheatsheaf Passage, Oxford, only to abruptly return and ruthlessly question Morse's involvement on their drink together in a studio set. As seen throughout the various episodes, opaque windows are a common occurrence when using studio settings or wishing to obscure the outside view.

With the musical notes of Tubular Bells playing loudly in the background, the scenes return to the centre of Oxford and the University. With the assumption of an uncle, innocuously calling to see his addicted nephew Ned, the town presents the gown and the first breathtaking views of the Magdalen College introduces the splendour of the Oxford Universities.

The founder of Magdalen College was William of Waynflete, the Bishop of Winchester. As his ambitions grew, he obtained permission from Henry VI to take over the buildings and lands of an ancient and decaying Hospital, where he established Magdalen College and its associated Hall and School. Established in the 17th century it continues its connection with the Physic Garden on the south side of Magdalen Bridge, which is today the Oxford Botanic Garden. Magdalen has some of the most hauntingly beautiful buildings of Oxford and sits amid a hundred acres of woodlands, riverside walks, and lawns.

Amongst the grounds is the famous Deer Park with the College's three hundred year old herd and grounds that contain fifty-seven species of birds.

Notably, one tradition is at sunrise on May morning the Magdalen Choir, whose foundation goes back to the very early years of the College, welcomes in the spring from the Great Tower.

The first cameo glimpse of Dexter as he passes Morse in the cloisters provided another foretaste of what was to become a habitual occurrence throughout the series.

It is hardly surprising that the initial location manager's role of presenting a photograph suggesting a location was easy.

With the stunning lighting, scenery, and white stone buildings, it was an ideal photogenic area. It was also at Magdalen College that Morse questions Ned.

On Morse's second visit to the now blinded Ned, the propinquity of the Radcliffe Infirmary to Jericho is only a matter of being a door away. The stunning use of lighting is evident in the expressive ambiance of the script set in the clinical surroundings. The Radcliffe Infirmary is a hospital in central Oxford, named after John Radcliffe. The Radcliffe Infirmary first opened in 1770 , being Oxford's first hospital. In 1758, the Radcliffe Trustees discussed the initial proposals to build a hospital in Oxford. An agreed donation of four thousand pounds for the new hospital saw it constructed on land given by Thomas Rowney, the Member of Parliament for Oxford.

Whilst Ned visits the chemist, the Thames provides the view from Adele Richardson's window at house in Bray. As Adele is obviously troubled, smoke wafts across the scene from an unseen cigarette.

It is whilst Morse attends the Richards lecture, that Jackson begins plotting a comfortable existence courtesy of Mr. Richards. Certainly, he is eagerly anticipating a more personally lucrative transaction on discussing his recorded observations of Anne's house during the Richard's visits than those of Inspector Morse.

Morse arrives at Magdalen College via Longwall Street, Oxford for Richard's lecture.

The inside scenes, though, are at the chapel, Royal Holloway Sanatorium. Note how the audience for the lecture looking remarkably similar to the choir in initial scenes! As Morse leaves the lecture, he again appears at the exit in Longwell Street, Oxford. Not only has Morse seemingly gone from Surrey to Oxfordshire, but also as a police car with sirens blazing answers an emergency call in Jericho, it somehow manages to go completely the wrong way by doubling back past Morse and back out on the same road.

However, scenes from St Aldates Police Station, did find the police at the correct location in Oxford.

Having approved a liberal payment from Mr. Richards, Jackson furiously cycles to pick up his blackmail money at a pre arranged destination. He peers apprehensively over the windswept buttercups.

Ideally placed near Bray Studios, Dorney Common, part of the Dorney Estate, Berkshire provides both the openness and solitude necessary for the venture. The Dorney Estate grew the original English Pineapple, so giving the name to the nearby Pineapple Pub. As discovered in the earlier chapter 'Meet the Boys' it also provided the ideal spot for the posting of a football coupon as an invasion of half-dressed crew invades the quiet of the common and filming commences.

The expanse of common land made larger by camera angles, it does provide a perfect location for the illicit deal. It enables Jackson to be easily observed freely absconding and furiously cycling back home in Oxfordshire -within seconds, quite an achievement for a cyclist! Without even being out of breath, he stops at a shop opposite the Oxford University Press Building in Jericho.

Then, shortly afterwards, effortlessly arrives outside his home, basket brimming with smuggled goods.

With great delight in his copious contraband, Jackson settles to enjoy his dividend. Morse and Lewis later inspect the evidence of his merchandise and the lewd evening's entertainment in its entirety.

The inquest for Anne sees a return to the Royal Sanatorium and Morse learns of her pregnancies and the outcomes. Little else is explained by the note left in a fishing rod at Jackson's, although it should perhaps of been questioned as to why the letter was at Jackson's rather than questioning the policeman who found it, or indulging in the admiration of the rod!

Enjoying a pint together for Lewis's birthday sees Morse and Lewis discussing the relevance of Oedipus Rex in the close proximity of the Bookbinder's Arms, Jericho.

The concluding scenes return to the houses in Canal Reach where a rapidly faltering Morse questions the remaining suspects. In the background, the sound of an airplane flying low is heard, the legacy of filming at the studio in Bray.

An unruffled Lewis walks past an opaque window to enter the house and save the day with a polite greeting. The ultimate closing scenes of this episode echoing the start as the shortly to become infamous Morse's jag again becomes the impenetrable obstacle to a villainous escape .So television history has made its mark on the British public and an era begins.

Also used for filming:-

Magdalen College has noticeably been the location for Wilde (1997), Howard's End (1992), Shadowlands (1993) and Henry VIII (1997), A Fish Called Wanda (1998) Hercule Poirot and Jack the Ripper, amongst others.

Blackwell's Bookshop featured in Treasure Hunt (1983).

THE SILENT WORLD OF NICHOLAS QUINN.

Aired on the 13th January 1987

Executive Producer Ted Childs

Producer Kenny McBain

Director Brian Parker

Production Designer David McHenry

Location Manager Russell Lodge.

Writers – Novel Colin Dexter. Julian Mitchell.

2.

Already a steadfast favourite the episodes continue with The Silent World of Nicholas Quinn.

The consequence of Nicholas Quinn's malfunctioning hearing aid at Oriel College, complete with the obligatory cameo role by Colin Dexter, provides the opening chain and again sets the mood for Oxford. Nicholas Quinn and Ogleby primarily emerge at the entrance to Oriel College and go out onto the front quad. They covertly discuss trepidation over the syndicate's malpractice, this later becoming an equally lethal judgment for both the individuals.

Founded in 1324 by Adam de Brome, Oriel is the fifth oldest of Oxford's Colleges. Built following the plague in the 14th century, it was the last to admit women. In later years, it is at Oriel that the Lollards became active.

The sweeping shots of St Mary the Virgins and All Souls College to Headington implies the venue for the Syndicate's HQ as Headington, with the realism of St John's Beaumont Rex School, Surrey genuinely veiled.

St. Mary's the Virgin is considered one of the oldest university buildings in the world with Church Architecture from the 13th century)Henry Chichele, the Archbishop of Canterbury, established all Souls College, The College of all Souls of the Faithful Departed, in 1438. King Henry VI was its formal co founder.

At St John's Beaumont Rex School, Surrey the urgent fire alarms reverberate through the corridors as the syndicate headquarters evacuates its employees.

One individual is fleetingly noticed trailing in his response before a glimpse of Morse's' House is seen at Castle Bar, Ealing. Now redeveloped as offices, it was initially a flat on a long-term lease to the television company.

Familiar locations rematerialize as the scenes transform to the cinema, Oxford University Press Buildings and shops in Jericho. Monica is hastily surveying bicycles to avoid recognition by Dr. Bartlett as he demonstrates a cool curiosity in the Parisian Film Industry.

Roope is also busy ascertaining his alibi at Oxford Railway Station, with Dedylus. Both later enter the Syndicate, although unaware of each other. Discovering the caretakers concern over unlocked drawers, cinema tickets, and keys warrants an explanation. As does, why Nicholas Quinn is absent from work. Both Morse and Lewis are also interested in Quinn's nonappearance subsequent to a call from an uneasy colleague, Donald Martin. Nicholas Quinn's house is a return to Dorney, Berkshire and the unique, small church at Boveney is in the background.

The present owners were not in residence at the time of filming Morse. However, recently it was a location in Midsommer Murders (the two series often-using similar locations). It is interesting that the house appears again later in the episode.

The principal aspect is the back doorway access befitting Nicholas Quinn's address. The narrow road is duly quiet and concealed for Morse to drive along. The house has parking opposite for a conservation area, ideal for parking the associated multitude of filming vehicles.

The residents adjacent to Dorney Common remember the busy scenes with the film crew arriving, although with the jaguar arriving on a trailer, rather than being driven. In the early series, the jaguar was not fully functional and what seemed like a high-speed chase was often on a trailer or with the jaguar pushed by several crewmembers.

The television company throughout filming owned the Jaguar Mk II, registration 248 RPA, offering it at the end to John Thaw, who declined the offer. James Went, from Oxford, then primarily won the jaguar in a competition. From here, a new owner put the jaguar in for restoration at Royale's a family vintage car restoration firm in the North of England since 1956.

The car took three years to restore, normally it would take two, but financial wrangling, concerning the new owner, stretched this to three years. Although the car was driveable and looked presentable, it was in poor condition at the time. Continuously patched and cosmetically enhanced with plastic filler three quarters of an inch thick in places, the bodywork of the car needed to be prepared, primed, and repainted. Stripped to a bare body-shell and as the paint was stripped, new evidence of old repairs and patches became apparent. New panels and paintwork replaced damaged and corroded parts. The panels replaced using original jaguar practice where appropriate. Adding a new vinyl roof was to restore the 'Morse' specifications. A 2.4 jaguar, referred to in the trade as a poor man's relation, would not have left the factory with a vinyl roof. Mechanically, the car was exhausted and in need of a complete overhaul. All mechanical components were reconditioned, replaced, or repaired. The engine fully rebuilt, converted to run on unleaded petrol. New glass and rubber seals, interior woodwork, upholstery, and carpets completed the renovation. Throughout the Morse series when the car door shuts, the tinny sound betrays the lack of felting to stop the window rattling. It was apparent an A frame was attached to the bodywork for towing the car whist filming. In June 2005, the car passed the MOT with flying colours and following a recent highly publicized auction, the fully restored car is now available for hire from its new owner.

Throughout filming the mirror is removed when the actors need to be seen and occasionally the windscreen. Tax discs also appear and disappear.

(Photographs kindly provided by David A C Royle & Co Ltd)

The tranquil Tudor residence resurfaces later, as Dr. & Mrs. Bartlett's abode, perfect for filming schedules. The angles of the detached house and the diverse areas easily allow multipurpose use and although some changes are evident over the years, the fishpond and white balustrade unmistakably linger as validation.

(Photo's Courtesy of the House Owner)

Investigating the scene results in perceiving a chair placed in a draft as curious. An opened sherry bottle with one glass becomes questionable. Additional facts from the cleaner consequently question debatable reasons why Quinn would buy salted butter.

Lewis begrudgingly opens a bottle of sherry at Morse's house pouring a glass for himself and the Inspector. He remains resentful when finding that as he sips his alone, he is supposedly sipping cyanide. The second untouched glass once washed, leaves an unopened bottle of sherry and a solitary glass. Regardless of a further drink with Monica at the Horse and Trumpet been filmed in the Postmasters House, Merton Street, Oxford, (not a pub) Morse is still significantly a long way from piecing the final parts of the jigsaw together.

It is at Brasenose that Morse probes Roope and Lewis later pursues Roope from the quad, through the Old and Chapel Quads and out onto Radcliffe Square. Roope then emerges in the Fellows Quad at Exeter, departing into Brasenose Lane. Lewis is on surveillance from above at Exeter's fellow gardens.

Still situated in its original location on Turl Street, Exeter College was founded in 1314 by Walter de Stapeldon of Devon, Bishop of Exeter and later treasurer to Edward II, who intended it as a school to educate clergy.

Lewis then emerges from St Edmund Hall, into the high street passing Roope on his imminent exit from the magna gallery. Roope then goes into the Botanical gardens.

In the intervening time, Morse is walking through to St Mary's Quadrangle at Oriel College before calling in on Ogleby's House and conferring over crossword clues. One of the houses visited, Ogleby's entails a trip to Old Windsor, Berkshire. Found in a secluded cul de sac with East Berkshire College nearby able to supply the parking, it is ideal. One point of note is when the ambulance rushes off, it turns into a dead end road. Making any hope of rapid medical attention purely fictional!

Next visiting Dr Bartlett's house, his son's emotional adoration of Wagner entertains Morse despite a phone call suspending the impromptu concert. The interior filming at Dr Bartlett's shows Richard conducting the recording of Wagner as Mrs. Bartlett's is on a gallery trying to attract his attention. The venue changes at this point to the gallery room at Dorney Court, Berkshire.

This is not a surprising venue, as Dorney Estate is renowned to location mangers. Essentially, Dorney Court offers an unrivaled local knowledge of forty years in the locations industry. It is an established preferential location for countless multinational filming organizations.

Dorney Court is the Palmer Family Home. The Estate famously displays uninterrupted panoramas over 100 acres of private grounds, containing both woodland and farmland. It offers unparallel opportunities with privacy, security, and freedom from external distractions. Most importantly, it presents the ability to portray many locations. Discreetly situated major companies may be recording at any given time, yet residents to the area may remain oblivious to the existing events. As a location, Dorney Court offers three and a half film-sets within one place.

Internally, it stages a galleried hall and paneled rooms with appropriate furniture, unique tapestries, a considerable anthology of collected works of art and antique artifacts

As the storyline continues, Monica dwells on recent events at the Radcliffe Infirmary. Morse is eager to arrest Roupe at the inquest in The Royal Sanatorium, Surrey before he realizes he has it wrong, and a mistake that results in a frenzied attack leaving Morse wounded. Rescued from crucial injury by a classic Lewis statement, it remains a memorable occasion.

Ever grateful, Morse offers to take Lewis to the cinema. Sadly, though it is a solitary lament at missing his Parisian tango as Lewis jubilantly delights at Jericho's cinemas choice of a family orientated film. Morse is left heading off for the preverbal thirst-quencher at the Jericho Tavern, possibly debating how many halves of cinema tickets were around the Oxford area that day and whether he should have asked to see Donald Martin's ticket earlier.

Also used for filming:-

Oriel College has been the location for Framed (2006).The house on the Dorney Court Estate provided a location in Midsommer Murders. Dorney Court has been the setting for Midsummer Night Murders (1997), Sliding Doors (1998), Miss Marples (2004), Poirot (2003), Elizabeth I, the Virgin Queen (2004) and Tess of the Ubervilles (1998), amongst numerous others.

THE SERVICE OF ALL THE DEAD

Aired on the 20th January 1987

Executive Producer Ted Childs

Producer Kenny McBain

Director Peter Hammond

Production Designer David McHenry

Location Manager Russell Lodge.

Writers – Novel Colin Dexter. Julian Mitchell.

3.

The instantly recognizable panoramic views over Oxford sweep down through the greenery and emerge with views of a small church nestled in a quiet countryside location. Another common ploy is evident to suggest the setting is Oxford, found in the Oxford 'For Sale' signs.

Idyllic until murder after murder evolves around families, church, and clergy. From gambling to child abuse, drunken tramps lurking behind gravestones and blackmailing brotherly vicars. The ghostly murders continue. The identity of a person long since acknowledged as dead remains concealed for now. Yet, in a seemingly normal home upstairs, murder, and mystery lurks beneath.

The truth does eventually emerge from the sinister bottomless cellars, although, for a while even a besotted Morse fails to recognize the ghostly companion of the target of his desires. Instead, he uncharacteristically refuses a drink and leaves without even glancing at him. The location for the drink was later to become significant as the place where Morse announces his first name.

This scene was at The Crown at Bray, a four hundred year old pub that is reputedly the most haunted in Britain. The church used was St Michael's Church at Bray, Berkshire.

Bray Church has a demonic legend attached to its history. The original church in the parish of Bray used to stand at Builderswell, the area around the Monkey Island. Allegedly in the fourteenth century the Queen saw the building whilst out with a hunting party from Windsor Castle. The old church looked very tumble-down and neglected, so the Queen then suggested replacing the church to the Bishop. The Bishop of Salisbury inspected the Church and ordered the structure's demolition. Workers then set about building a new one in a gothic style on the same spot. The beginnings of the new edifice rose high above ground as work quickly progressed. In the morning, the poor workers found nothing but a pile of wood and stone. Puzzled they had no alternative but to start again.

When this happened night after night, the situation became quite impossible and so the church officials felt the only way to overcome the demons was to move the site of the church to somewhere else in the parish and give prayers to St. Michael who gained fame by defeating the Devil. The builders moved the site for the church to the ford at Bray. However, The Bishop had only allocated a certain amount of money and with so much work destroyed there was no longer enough to complete the church.

The Bishop's representatives called a meeting with the local villagers to discuss the situation. After much deliberation, the people of Bray agreed that they would raise the money to build the church, so long as the diocese would pay for the construction of a chantry chapel. Finally, Bray's church was completed and feeling that St. Michael had heard their prayers, they dedicated it in his honour. Round behind the church the Bishop had the chantry chapel built just as promised. An Old Saxon carving of a dog from the church at Builderswell remains in the wall as a reminder of the problems they had faced.

A gothic feel shrouds a serene Oxfordshire as Peter Hammond's unique reflective style dominates the filming. The setting for the shooting of this episode was heavily reliant upon being able to use a church near Bray Studios, with St Mary's at Bray being the third church considered. The episode abandonment planned if the team had received a refusal at this point. Fortunately, the Vicar was willing to discuss it after watching filming at the library, at nearby Huntercoombe Manor.

The library scenes at Huntercoombe Manor appear later, when Morse and the Archbishop discuss details of the case. Watching the filming meant he had access to judge the intrusiveness the filming may have on normal church activities.

The bell-ringer briefly seen in one of the opening shot was not from Bray Church. However, the Bray Bell ringers have appeared recently in Midsommer Murders also filmed at Bray Church. The church scenes for Midsommer murders were at Bray as the nearby village scenes were at The Lee, which did not have a village church. The church itself was at Monks Risborough, Buckinghamshire. The bell ringers moved from one location to another to preserve continuity

On agreement, the location of St. Michael's of Bray became St Oswald's in The Service of All the Dead.

Morse comes out of Blackwell's opposite the Sheldonian, Oxford and giving the estimated time of arrival as twelve minutes, he speeds off towards Bray, Berkshire.

The crew convened for a total of three weeks, every day's work reputedly equaling one minute of filming. The location manager was always working two weeks ahead on locations at this time. During the three weeks spent filming, normality restored at the weekends to allow for services and three weddings to continue. The crew would quite happily arrive on a Sunday afternoon, complete with families and picnics, and then set up on a Sunday night for the weeks filming. Each Friday night all of the props went into one corner and covered by curtains.

As the scenes move inside the church and wailing widows are comforted, the parishioners verify Joseph's body. The dead body was at Bray, but in the church hall, which is within the grounds. This was partly for purposes of space, mainly though because the shutters on the arched window gave exactly the right lighting.

As the trail evolves, they continue to look for the missing figure of the vagrant. However, unlike the parishioners, the police are unaware the tramp was closer than once thought.

The detectives then revisit the church and Lewis goes in search of the vicar. The guilt ridden religious man, however, is looming ever closer to the ground.

Morse in the churchyard and the eighty-foot high tower at Bray, in all its glory, provided impressive shots for the dramatic exodus of the vicar. Although the stuntman was willing to do the scene, the producer felt unable to validate the insurance costs for a solitary shot. It transpired that spikes around the tower became the main difficulty regarding health and safety, for the stuntman. A dummy sufficed as the body, a bike placed underneath the cadaver for the next shot. Extra props supplemented the tower to fit the bill on finding a corpse on the church's rooftops. However, the outstanding views across the River Thames from the tower were genuine, even if Morse's fear of heights did not allow him to have the benefit of them! Many of the camera crew echoed his sentiments on the day. The roof is actually aluminum. The crew covered this whilst filming giving it the look of a lead roof and supplying a sturdier footing for the crew needed on the roof for filming. The crew also fitted the stairwell with a chain to act as a banister, which they left in situ. Initially offered to Bray church props brought in for the inside of the church-such as altar rails and religious artifacts were for use in a high church and so were sent to a high church in Reading, Berkshire.

Interestingly, the local villagers were aware of the filming, but not what each day would bring. One such villager was returning home and as they pulled into the lane, they saw the body plummet from the tower. Taken aback, it took a moment to realize it was the filming. The flapping white robes descending from the tower caused a moments alarm. Finally realizing what was happening, they watched the unceremonious hauling of the saintly spirit back up to the top for a repeat performance.

The church's interior modification was radical, so much so that the Diocese did not recognize the church when it appeared on film (for comparison the same church in its unadulterated grandeur appears later in the episode entitled Dead on Time). Confession boxes, pulpits and many different props appeared and to all intent and purposes, it would be testing for anyone to comprehend the original. A few other areas at Bray were used, the boiler house area for the drunks (with a few extra props), the iron gate, the lynch gate that Ruth is seen rather hurriedly cycling towards and views down into the village of Bray.

Morse and Lewis drive over Marlow Bridge and a riverside flat is from this area.

For Ruth's house a cellar was a prerequisite to represent, the hidden depths that a wheelchair bound mother could not probe. For that reason, a house near Wimbledon was eventually found to fit the bill, however for her place of work the location returns to nearer Bray Studio and to the informal Dorney Court.

The introduction of written examinations in 1800 and the restriction on Dons being marrying lifted in 1870; saw an increased interest in the University and the building of the large houses on Woodstock road. The Dons being free to marry envisaged large families. The large houses resembled the architecture of houses in and around Ealing, London, and these suggested houses in Woodstock road during filming.

65

As mentioned, a second church provided some locality shots with the team transferring filming to Hurley, a tranquil village in Berkshire. One small part did return to Bray, the entrance to the crypt was at Bray, but the crypt itself at Hurley. Founded in the mid 11th century, Hurley Priory was a memorial to the first wife of the great Norman Lord, Geoffrey De Mandeville.

The church door at Hurley comes into view as Morse arrives to converse with Dr Starkey about the diversity between a brotherly Vicar and a Tramp. The house visited is adjacent to the church itself.

Morse and Lewis visit The Turf Tavern is a historic pub located just outside the Oxford city walls. With foundations dating back to the 14th century, its city centre location makes it a favourite for both town and gown. It is here Morse refuses a drink seeing Ruth, but fails to realize she is with Harry Josephs. The carnage of bodies continues - the most in the series and Hurley was the location for the body found by a willow tree.

It is whilst at Bray Church – supposedly in Oxford, that the sound of an airplane at low altitude suggests it is somewhat lost in Oxford! It is in Oxford, however, that Morse goes into Lloyds Bank. This is now the tourist information centre in Oxford where tours are available around the colleges and a Morse Tour.

The college scenes are from Merton College, with its unique design of archways and it is at Merton College that Colin Dexter makes his cameo appearance.

Founded in 1264, and set in extensive gardens and grounds, Merton College is one of three ancient Oxford colleges founded in the thirteenth century. The College's founder was Walter de Merton, Lord Chancellor of England, and Bishop of Rochester. Merton College is one of many colleges embraced by the University of Oxford. The colleges are self-governing institutions that provide the teaching for most undergraduates, although the exam administration is by the university, which holds the sole power to award degrees.

Oxford served as the home base for King Charles I, during the Civil War, with the colleges giving most of their plate to Charles. From 1642 to 1646, Charles stayed at Christ Church, whilst Queen Henrietta held court at Merton College. Oxford suffered heavily for its support of Charles, Oliver Cromwell becoming the chancellor of the University in 1650, ordering the destruction of the city defense

Morse has little time to interrogate anyone further as he realizes what has been happening. As he conceals himself in a confession box, he overhears a confidential tête-à-tête that clarifies all. Somewhat misplaced rationalizing of moral intentions explain the misplaced tramp, initial murder, and ensuing massacre.

With a psychopath having agreed to the first murder, killing his wife, the man who had taken his wife and his son, the rest was easy. Certainly, the money was most welcome.

Now, with all in impeccable harmony with Inspector Morse and the case finally closed. Nothing then can surpass the delight at Morse and Lewis retiring for a drink at The Crown at Bray, apart from the remnants of a sore throat.

With the courtrooms for the inquest set in Ealing, Morse suggests that Ruth was about to confess all, so reducing her sentence.

With a strand of light streaming through the slightly opened door, gently the spotlight falls on Morse as Morse asks to visit her. The shadows fade and against the austere prison window outline they intimately entwine in a tender embrace.

Also used in Filming

Bray/Bray Studios is famous for many films, including Alien (1979), The Rocky Horror Picture Show (1975), Dracula (1958/1966), The Hound of the Baskervilles ((1959), The Curse of Frankenstein (1957), the Wolfman (1961), The Phantom of the Opera (1962), The Creeping Unknown (1959), The Mummy (1959), The Brides of Dracula (1960), The Abominable Snowman (1957), The Plague of the Zombies (1966) and many others

THE WOLVERCOTE TONGUE

Aired on the 25th December 1987

Executive Producer Ted Childs

Producer Kenny McBain

Directed by Alastair Reid.

Producer Kenny McBain

Production Designer David McHenry

Location Manager Russell Lodge.

Writers – Novel Colin Dexter. Julian Mitchell

4.

The long-established Oxford landscape seems undisturbed in contrast to the incoming bus full of American tourists outside The Randolph Hotel. The Randolph is a firm favourite of Colin Dexter's. Built in 1864 and recently refurbished, it offers the highest level of comfort and service in a traditional and welcoming environment. During filming, some of the actors soon admired it and it boasts a Morse Bar embracing a great deal of memorabilia from the series.

Briefly mentioned, the St Giles Fair is traditional street fair in September. Taking up the whole of St Giles, the town comes to a standstill as rides hurl riders within inches of the ancient buildings.

It is in this bar that Morse and Lewis confer, with Colin Dexter, Julian Mitchell, and Dr. Robert Gasser (Brasenose College Bursar) in the background, these being the novelist, screen- writer, and college advisor for the series. The bar was Chapters Bar at the time of filming, before becoming the Morse Bar.

A concierge does mention the appearance of external red carpets outside the hotel during Morse's time. It is also noticeable that Oxford's seemingly unpolluted buildings during filming now appear to have acquired an unfortunate additional coating of grime and filth in the present-day.

The opulence of the hotel is flawless and The Randolph as a location offers local parking in the quieter area of St Giles and an opportunity for effortless representation of landmarks such as the Martyrs Memorial and Ashmoleum Museum, amongst other Oxford architecture.

The region so ideally consigns the scenes as Oxford that the bordering area is a frequent backdrop as Morse manoeuvers the jaguar through the ancient urban sprawl. It is in St Giles that Morse screeches to a halt and issues an all port warning.

A weary and drained tour guide attempts to pacify the fatigued American tourists as the coach arrives at the Randolph. The plot pivots on the replacing of the legendary Wolvercote Tongue to its native soil and the dejected American tourists visit to Oxford undoubtedly leaves them with plenty of travelers tales to tell.

Gilbert Scott designed the Martyrs Memorial. During the Tudor period, Henry VIII took control of Christ Church from the founder Cardinal Wolsey. He abolished the study of cannon law and introduced Medicine, Civil Law, Greek, Theology and Hebrew. When his daughter Mary came to rule and tried to reverse the Anglican reform to Catholicism, many prominent leaders perished, hence the Protestant martyrs.

Nicholas Ridgley, Hugh Latimer, and Thomas Granburgh, respectively the Bishops of London, Worcester, and Canterbury, remained true to their protestant beliefs. The master of Balliol College in the 1360's was John Wycliffe whose published religious works forced his resignation as Master. His followers, known as Lollards, continued with his philosophical works.

The site of the burnings remains marked by a cross set in the pavement outside Balliol College, and the Martyr's Memorial at the corner of Broad and St. Giles commemorates the event. The set of doors hung between the quads of Balliol bear scorch marks from the fire.

The exceptional Ashmolean Museum develops into the stage setting as Theodore Kemp materializes and greets Shelia, only to tell her of the end of their affair. Ostentatious in character, Theo is cold and to the point, leaving Shelia reaching for the reassurance she finds in gin and tonic.

The Ashmolean Museum opened its doors on 24th May 1683, providing a setting in which a private collection emerged into the public domain. The museum is one of the oldest in Britain and amongst the treasures is the Alfred Jewel (donated in 1718). This became the inspiration for the Wolvercote Tongue.

As Theo and Cedric Downes meet with the tourists, they are unaware that one of the members of the team has died.

The pathologist convinced Mrs. Poindexter had died of natural causes, leaves to attend the annual dinner. Morse is not pleased and his manner of questioning leaves the pathologist an acid taste. Morse and Lewis do see the funny side though as the pathologist hurriedly dashes from the scene.

The tour continues, but following a medieval phone call Cedric replaces the now unavailable Theo. Poindexter, meanwhile, meets a long lost relative at Church Art, Ealing, West London. The sightseers are discouraged to find his forgetful narrating above the foundations of the surrounding architecture substandard. Cedric is seemingly preoccupied with events elsewhere as he guides the tour to the gardens at New College, Oxford.

However, it seems the body of one-character voyages even further afield to Surrey at Newark Priory.

Tumbling over a small weir, the naked body falls at the feet of a couple enjoying the riverside view. Lewis is convinced the body is that of Poindexter, only to find the exposed remains of Theo Kemp. Lewis departs to inform his widower whilst Morse informs his long-term lover.

Shelia stares through the bottom of her glass, the remains of the gin and tonic still glistening on her lips. Unable to believe the news that Morse has brought she seems inconsolable as she flings herself at Morse for comfort. Sobbing uncontrollably, she agrees not to mention the events of the night to anyone for the moment.

Theo's wife, wheelchair bound, confronts Lewis with a lively spirit. Thrown from the car driven by her husband whilst he had walked away unscathed, she was left a cripple. Theo had to remain by her side and care for her- it could never end. He owed it to her.

Like two bookends, Morse and Lewis adorn the sofa in Morse's home. A pint of beer in each hand the symmetrical raising and lowering to their lips mirror each other. Morse gets up to fetch a pint of milk as the dawn rises. Pondering the day's incidents, Morse sits with a pint of beer in one hand and a pint of milk in the other, despite Lewis yawning in a bid to escape the home decorating.

Poindexter's thoughts also seem to be elsewhere as he disappears, despite all port warnings and Harold Brown follows suit as he also disappears the next day, carefully tailed by the observant Lewis.

A phone call from Lewis provides a revelation for a bemused Morse who joins Lewis in the tourist sunshine. Consuming an ice-lolly, they watch whilst a satiated Harold Brown blissfully marvels at the evaporating era of working steam trains. Winding his way through contented sightseers at Didcot Steam Railway Museum, Morse stops Harold's enjoyment on a steam train footplate.

Didcot Railway Centre, Oxfordshire, boasts one of the finest collections of Great Western Railway steam locomotives, carriages, wagons and buildings in the country. The 23 acre site is based around the original engine shed built in 1932 and has been developed to show many aspects of GWR history. The Centre still has the original engine shed complete with coal stage, water columns, and turntable. Open to the public, steam journeys are available for the train enthusiast to Thomas the Tank rides for the younger fan.

Used as a filming location 100 times since 1983, Didcot Railway Museum is a prominent location mangers choice. Filming for The Wolvercote Tongue took place in 1987, the episode shown on television at 21.00 hrs on Christmas Day.

The team contacted the Museum months in advance regarding preparations for filming. A diagram was sent of where each camera would be filming from, a small track being laid and four engines ordered - two steaming and two not. Engine drivers were to be supplied and refreshments available from the on site café. The centre remained open to the public and anyone visiting that day was able to watch filming. Didcot staff is familiar with filming taking place and some volunteers are readily available as extras.

The cost for the day was three hundred and fifty pounds for the large engines and two hundred and fifty for the smaller ones. The film crew arrived the day before to prepare the area for filming and returned at 7.30 am the next day to commence filming at 8.30 am.

The intention of a sunny day thwarted by torrential rainfall meant some filming had to be inside. First engines 6106 and 6998 were steamed and ready to go, complete with three Didcot drivers and two firemen. Later seen as Oxford Station, an extra requested shot of a multiple unit train with the door opening was at Didcot because mainline trains cannot stop for filming.

The entourage was small and so able to park locally. The restaurant at the centre supplied all catering needs and a continuous supply of ice creams - a fresh one for each shot. John Thaw purchased a jar of marmalade for his wife, from one of the staff and Colin Dexter continues to do so. The marmalade has recently won a silver award in the U.K Taste Awards.

A local newspaper reporter's abiding memory of that day was of John Thaw. A professional actor trying to do his job was not so keen on irritating reporters!
Whenever John Thaw walked towards the reporter between takes, an effort to ask a few questions meant being ushered away by the entourage. Clearly, Mr. Thaw was not keen on giving any interviews at that point!

The photographer made a much better choice by chatting up the crew. This resulted in her actually getting permission to allow her onto the camera car, which they were using for tracking shots of John Thaw and Kevin Whately driving around the area. Quite candidly, she was sitting next to the camera operator clicking away. Whether this would still be possible with today's climate of risk assessment and health and safety - not to mention the more restraining influences of film and TV PR departments is debatable!

On leaving the location to drive back to the office with what had become a great picture story, the reporters noticed John Thaw and Kevin Whately repositioning the Jaguar, presumably for the next shot. Morse and Lewis were openly driving the Jaguar around the roads of Oxfordshire probably meaning quite a few double takes for any other people who noticed them that day!

Interestingly, as Morse and Lewis depart from Didcot , Lewis falls asleep in the car and the jaguar is seen driving the length of one expanse of the departing road only to shortly been seen driving back further up the road, the editing going back on itself.

It's marmalade and murder for Morse

THE riddle of the murdered American tourist and t missing Wolvercote Tongue jewel has got police baffled

An American woman has been found dead at the Randolph Hotel Oxford and, although a heart attack is suspected, Inspector Morse a his assistant Sergeant Lewis have other ideas.

If you think it sounds like something out of a television show, then you're right.

The great travelling circus of TV production came to Didcot railway centre with location sequences for the new Inspector Morse series starring John Thaw and Kevin Whately.

Fliss Coombs, of the company making the series, explained: "The inspector is brought in to unravel the murder and find the jewel.

"Everyone in the party of tourists comes under suspicion. Morse and Lewis have to keep tabs on the party and find themselves at the railway centre after one of the group turns out to be a railway enthusiast."

But for the 44-strong crew from Zenith Productions the day at

By MARK HELLINGS

Didcot turned into a wash-out.

Heavy rain for much of the d meant that most of the outd filming had to be hastily : scheduled for indoors.

Fliss said: "It caused us a fe continuity problems because should have been a nice sun day."

The railway centre stayed op and technicians and actor ingled with the sightseers w had come to see the steam engin

Jeanette Howse, of the cent said: "We told the company had to stay open and they did mind because they wanted to people milling around."

Later, Inspector Morse ca be seen driving Jaguar round Didco

As far actor Jo Thaw, his tough image slipped wh staff at the cen found his weaknes

Jeanette said: was quite taken v our jam.

"We pick apples and bl berries here make the j ourselves. He four pots home v him and a pot of marmalade."

STAR: John Thaw in Didcot

BRUSH-UP: Inspector Morse on the set

Zenith Productions Limited

Mrs. Jeanette Howse,
Didcot Railway Centre,
Didcot Station,
Didcot,
Oxon.   17th June, 19

Dear Mrs. Howse,

RE: "INSPECTOR MORSE" - SERIES #2

'Missing Pieces'

Thank you for your tentative acceptance of our proposed filming of th
above murder/mystery drama, at the Museum, between 23rd July and 26th
August, 1987.

I hope to be able, after our further visit with the Director Alastair
Reid, to finalise dates, requirements and facility fees at the earlie
opportunity.

Please do not hesitate to contact me should you have any queries or
anticipate any problems.

Meanwhile, thank you for your co-operation.

Yours sincerely,
PP ZENITH PRODUCTIONS LTD

RUSSELL LODGE
Location Manager

pc KMCB
   RF
   PS
   A/c

81

Morse and Lewis visit Cedric's wife, Lucy, at home to discuss the curtains amongst other details. Following her journey to London, the curtains prompt Morse and Lewis to revisit the house. Meanwhile, Mrs. Kemp's suicide, Morse visiting Shelia in the sculpture room at the Ashmoleum, Shelia's reaction and decision to tell Cedric all pay a part in the plot.

As Lucy enters the phone box outside of Paddington station to call her husband, she turns and smiles. Belatedly realizing the danger, she slides down the phone booth to lay crumpled on the floor.

Cedric waits patiently for his wife at Oxford station, turning as she fails to arrive. Lewis's persistence in questioning times causes Cedric to run into Poindexter's arms and leaves Morse questioning whom to arrest.

Poindexter had been in the room when his wife had died, he realized she was dead, what more could he do? Morse does suggest he should have called an ambulance, but it seems he had left her, thrown the Wolvercote tongue into the river so he could claim the insurance and rushed to be reunited with his only long lost child.

Cedric's story was a different tale, Theo had been visiting his wife, and Cedric had walked in on them. He had hit out at Theo who had fallen against the chimney suffering a fatal blow to the head. He had to kill Lucy; surely, Morse was able to understand? Now sullied, she was no longer untainted and pleasing to him. Morse is not as understanding as perhaps Cedric would have liked.

The day ending, Morse and Lewis watch a diver searching for the Wolvercote Tongue in the river alongside The Trout Inn, Oxford.

The daughter of Walter de Clifford, Rosamund was allegedly the mistress of King Henry II. Myth suggests that during his travels across England, King Henry stayed at The Trout Inn. In secret, he would signal his presence to Rosamund with a lantern in the window to the secret garden in which he kept her. Then Rosamund would to through an underground tunnel to The Trout and spend the night with her lover The only way through was by means of a silver thread and the gardens were defended by his Knight Sir Thomas.

In 1175, King Henry left to go to war with his son. Two stories suggest a feverishly envious Queen Eleanor killed Sir Thomas stealing the silver thread from him. Discovering her way through the maze, she finds Rosamund, and kills her by forcing her to drink from a poisoned chalice. Alternatively, that Queen Eleanor herself placed the lantern in the window while King Henry was away at war, and when Rosamund emerged from the secret tunnel, she killed her with a dagger. Rosamund is well- known locally as The White Lady and visits the Trout regularly. She walks on the original floor of The Trout, which has since had additional flagstones added to it (stones taken from the ruins of Godstow Nunnery), and therefore is only seen from the knee up.

As Morse and Lewis wait patiently, slowly raising from the depths of the river a diver's hand reaches skywards. With the Wolvercote Tongue held aloft as a trophy, the scene is reminiscent of Excalibur. The case now closed, Lewis goes off to see Aunt Sissy. Morse, however, informs Lewis he prefers to watch fishes – through the bottom of a beer glass.

Also used in Filming

Didcot railway museum is no stranger to filming and apart from Inspector Morse, Carrie's War (2004), Treasure Hunt (1983) and Trains with Peter Waterman, to mention a few used the museum as a location.

LAST SEEN WEARING

Aired on the 8th March 1988

Executive Producer Ted Childs

Producer Kenny McBain

Director Edward Bennett

Production Designer David McHenry

Assistant Location Manager Martin Lee

Writers – Novel Colin Dexter. Thomas Ellice.

5.

Magdalen Bridge fades into The Museum of the History of Science and on to the Sheldonian, suggesting the peace and quiet of academic Oxford. In extreme contrast, Morse is disturbed from reflective mood by the boisterous commotion of builders outside his home. Already irate, the shrill call of the telephone is enough to drive Morse into desperation. Strange demanding to see Morse immediately leads to an explanation of the flu and a missing person for Morse to uncover.

Lewis is awaiting Morse's arrival, already primed with the files of Valerie Craven, he is eager to find the missing girl. Exasperated by Morse's sluggish pace, Lewis is sure the girl is still alive, whereas Morse is adamant Valerie is dead.

In search of the missing girl, Morse and Lewis arrive at Bluecoats School, Sonning, Berkshire, where, inquiring about Valerie they discover she is a typical teenager, full of melancholy and rage.

Sonning's status as site of the palace of the Bishops of Salisbury appears to have its roots in the reign of Edward the Elder (899-924). Sonning remained the site of the Bishop's Palace (at Holme Park, now Reading Bluecoat School) until 1574. Reading Blue Coat School is located on the edge of the village in Holme Park, formerly owned by the Palmer family ("not the biscuits!"), who were great benefactors of the village.

The filming took place during the summer recess, the school being a school for boys, not girls as portrayed. For the scenes at the school, all extras were actors brought in for the filming. Morse and Lewis approach the school down Sonning Lane, off the A4, where they turn into the school a bus stop is in the background. The bus stop is no longer there, the area now the home of the Sonning Cricket and Hockey Club. As Morse and Lewis turn into the school, they stop to look at a hockey pitch. This is actually a cricket field and as Morse and Lewis seemingly appraise the hockey match, they have actually repositioned the car.

The actors are looking away from the cricket field, down a sloping passageway, fading into a dead end. Despite the actual view sloping down, both actors eye line remain inline with the hypothetical hockey match taking place.

The maneuvering continues as the car appears by the hockey pitch, at one point the pair look out of the car window to the left, whereas a long view shot suggests they should have been looking to the right.

As Morse and Lewis walk into the school, to the left of Lewis, is a statue of a Bluecoat Boy. A famous school in Dorset, the Bluecoat school used to send second hand uniforms to the Blueboys of Sonning. Ahead there is a clock where there is normally a bowl of flowers. Concealed lighting equipment cleverly tucked behind corners remains hidden from view as Morse, Lewis and Miss Baines continue into the school. They walk through the entrance hall and into the secretary's office, which in reality is the headmaster's office.

The office is now complete with a tallboy, brought in as a prop. As Morse and Lewis walk out by a line of hedges, the weather is dull and dreary. Extensive lighting of a bank of fifteen lights shining directly onto them, complete with generator, gave the impression of a sunny day. The intensity of the lights shines intently on Morse's suit. They drove the jaguar whilst there and as Morse and Lewis drive off they drive towards the stable block where there is no way out. The scenes with Cheryl and the Headmaster were in the school grounds, but the headmasters' home was not (possibly, filmed at Bearwood College, Wokingham, Berkshire). It is the main hall at the school that Miss Baines introduces the girls to Morse and Lewis. The filming was planned and restoration work on a recently flood -damaged paneled wall was due to finish in time. As the day of filming loomed nearer, the work was nowhere near completed. On contacting the company, the panic was short lived as the art and design crew stepped in and restored the room to its former glory with the aid of props and theatrical paint. Artistic plaques of horses completely covered the damaged panels. Around the area, the team repaired and stained the woodwork, leaving the work when they left. The marble fireplace behind Morse and Lewis is in the main hall, as they are. The girls they are talking too are on chairs brought in from the staff room to the common room.

At no point were the girls, Morse, and Lewis in the same room during the ensuing conversation between them. Not seen together on film, the shots of the conversation go from one scene to another, the two pieces of film joined later in post production.

Cheryl Baines is with a student in the buttery, the blackboard is a prop as are all the desks. A filing cabinet is an added prop to block off a door. Cheryl Baines and the Headmaster are in the chapel, the computer, pictures and desk being props. The stained glass windows exist but the colours intensified for filming and later Morse talks to Liz Hurley in the garden, waking past the chapel.

Enough learnt Morse and Lewis hurriedly escape to the local pub. Just after time, a hurried retreat sends Lewis to the supermarket for replacements that fall short of Morse's approval in London.

Craven Builders are undertaking the building of the M40 and Morse meets with the boss, Valerie's father. With alarming descriptions, he recalls events and suggests Morse reads the files, as he does not intend to repeat himself.

Asking Morse if he is the drinker, Morse responds, "I don't know, are you the tyrant?" Evidently, a clash of personality is to emerge, not only with Morse and Craven, but also with Phillipson and Cheryl Baines.

A letter from Valerie rekindles Lewis's resolve that Valerie is alive. Not only alive, but also living with John Maguire in SW3, Morse wonders if Valerie could be hiding under the bed as previous searches had revealed nothing. Nevertheless, they travel to London in pursuit. With Morse despondent that he cannot arrest Maguire for his bad taste, at his home in Chenye Walk, Chelsea, they continue to search the contemporary apartment. Morse's nose becoming a bit "sniffy" means a trip to Chelsea harbour to check Maguire involvement and a return to Bluecoat school to question the girls about diaries and crushes.

With a description of agreeable men narrowing to a list of Accombe, who has left and Donald, the headmaster, Donald is the nearest to be questioned.

A family home complete with the functional unit of the ideal wife, husband and two children, all seems reliably harmless. A loving couple, as one starts a sentence the other finishes it. Helpfully, they direct Morse to Accombe's school – not in Reading as suggested, but Marston, Oxford.

A cursory chat with Accombe means stopping for a quick drink before they are on their way to question the Cravens house in Surrey. At the villa, they broke a chip off the interior marble staircase, which did not go down well at all! Finally,

Morse travels to Sonning, Berkshire and to Cheryl Baines's house. With the love of houses on corners to give depth of field, Sonning provided an impressive bend in the road.

Surprisingly, Morse is seen buying food at Nisa supermarket, London, whilst discussing the case with Lewis, but the obligatory whiskey is nestled amongst the cornflakes, coffee, and biscuits.

More amazingly, to Lewis, Morse admits to fraudulent letter writing.

The familiar arrival of a visitor to Cheryl, hints of raised voices and a fall leaves Donald concerned as she fails to arrive at school the next day. The screams of a housekeeper surveying Cheryl's torn and twisted body gently fade into scene denoting a full police attendance, with Lewis tersely responding to Morse's questions and Strange smelling not only a flaw in the detective's work, but whiskey in the coffee mug. Morse is in trouble, not only with strange but with George Craven, despite his natural haired wife being a little more responsive. Lewis, meanwhile, recreates a visitor to Cheryl's flat, a scene yet again recreated by Christchurch Gate to Oriel Square, Oxford following Morse's visit to Christchurch library. With a flurry of arrests following, as often is the case, Lewis's remark about Catholics signifies the need for a lift home for David Accombe.

Despite a bid to conceal the evidence, the masked face is unpeeled and reveals the true Valerie Craven. Further truths emerge back at the Craven house and as the infidelities unfold, honesty prevails and Morse's competent conclusions close the case.

With the sunlight flickering through the trees, the polished sheen of the jaguar unhurriedly drives along the country lane. Slowly it vanishes from view as it disappears into a shallow dip in the road.

THE SETTLING OF THE SUN.

Aired on the 15th March 1988

Executive Producer Ted Childs

Producer Kenny McBain

Director Peter Hammond

Production Designer David McHenry

Location manager Russell Lodge

Writers – Novel Colin Dexter. Charles Wood.

6.

The opening scenes show the Bodleian library, Old Schools Quad. The Bodleian Library Oxford, England, known informally to centuries of Oxford scholars as "the Bod", opened in 1602 with a collection of 2000 books assembled by Thomas Bodley of Merton College.

It is in Exeter College that an old man sits in a wheelchair with stigmatic marks to the palms of his hands. As a young girl tenderly holds these hands, Morse walks to join her. Together they wheel the reverend figure across Magdalen Bridge, before retracing their steps and arriving at the Botanical gardens.

As the elderly man falls to sleep, Morse and the girl, Jane, stroll through the grounds of the Botanical Gardens. With great agility amongst the Japanese voices, the elderly Reverend Robson flees the constrictions of his wheelchair and bounds into the hothouse. His intention in the panic is to attack the Japanese girl, as he strives forward he collapses as he reaches her.

The scenes change to the Radcliffe Camera.

Coach loads of tourists are arriving at Brasenose College, courtesy of Pearce's coaches. They are greeted by Thomas at the reception, although one in particular by Mrs. Warbut. With a glaring momentary look and bombarded by the strains of Mrs. Warbut's fluent Japanese, the visitor enters his room.

The dining hall accommodates the guests for a later supper and talk. Morse proudly judges the crossword competition and presents the prize, interrupted by Yukio Lee collapsing. With concern flying, the later horror of finding Yukio Lee killed in a ceremonial style affects the majority of the onlookers. Lewis, however, remains more concerned at the lack of blood given the sheer brutality of the murder. Morse remains squeamish and Jane snappy as they pass through the gym on route to the bursary. As the punch bag swings freely, the sound of dripping water from the taps in the shower room shortly register in Morse's curiosity. Stopping fleetingly, he then joins Jane to walk across Brasenose New Quad to the Bursary. Morse's inquisitiveness continues as he spots a photograph of Singapore huddled beside Mrs. Warbut's teabags. Relentlessly torn apart Pearce's coaches answer many questions and interrogations. Pearce's driver Peter Bennett appeared in the filming and took the coach to Denham Studios.

During filming the crew took several seats out of the coach and changed the lighting to film police searching, they then replaced all the seats and lighting before leaving.

96

Drugs and false Germans seem to be the order of the day, sending Morse and Lewis in search of a drink.

As they turn and walk under Hertford Bridge an adeptly witty scene of a drunk, walking backwards, seems to sum up their feelings before they arrive at the Turf Tavern.

Graham Daniels has unexpected company at the college, although he is next seen in the toilets outside the Guildhall in London.

Jane, meanwhile, is playing croquet on the lawns at the Monkey Island Hotel, Bray, Berkshire, before joining Morse at his home and explaining she never really had any feelings for him.

Monkey Island, near the village of Bray-on-Thames lays one-mile down-stream from Maidenhead. Often assumed that the Island takes its name from the monkey paintings in the pavilion, however the name derives from the earlier title of *"Monks Eyot"* indicating that the island was being used by Monks, probably in association with their fishery in the Thames. The monks in question resided at Amerden Bank, near Bray Lock on the Buckinghamshire bank of the river, where a cell of Merton Priory was in existence from 1197 until the Dissolution.

In about 1723, Charles Spencer, the 3rd Duke of Marlborough, purchased the island and by 1840, the pavilion had become a riverside Inn, reached by ferry from the South bank.

Together with Max's explanation for the lack of blood at Yukio Li's murder scene, Morse realizes he is the perfect witness. Sir Wilfred as Jeremy Owens father, Friedman as Jane's brother and a misunderstanding about the need to frame Yukio Li as member of a drugs syndicate all lead to confusion. With Morse as a perfect witness to Yukio Li's murder leaves Yukio Li in a revengeful mode and Morse has to rush to save Jane.

This achieved, Morse is next at Exeter College Chapel discussing morals issues with Mrs. Warbut. He later joins Jane's grandniece and takes flowers to the Radcliffe Infirmary for the recuperating Jane.

THE LAST BUS TO WOODSTOCK

Aired on the 22nd March 1988

Executive Producer Ted Childs

Producer Kenny McBain

Director Peter Duffell

Production Designer David McHenry

Assistant Location Manager Martin Lee

Writers – Novel Colin Dexter. Micheal Wilcox

7.

Irrevocable credence to the vicinity of Oxford as the perceived location occurs from Pembroke Square, with outlooks bordering the eminent Tom Tower on a ferocious, wet, and stormy night.

Tom Tower as part of Christ Church College, houses the bell Great Tom. To this day, the bell rings one hundred and one times at 21:05 GMT (9 o'clock p.m. solar time) every night for the one hundred and one original scholars of the college. In former times, this signaled the close of all the college gates throughout Oxford.

The arena swiftly alters from rain falling to a puddle in a plausible Woodstock Road, Oxfordshire. In reality Old Beaconsfield, Buckinghamshire permits the essential elongated prospect of a bus arriving and coincidental arrival of a willing driver both journeying towards Woodstock.

In contrasting reality, the car pulls into the Fox and Castle Public House, Old Windsor, Berkshire. It is here that the tale of murder instigated within the confines of the Fox & Castle car park unravels. The pub becomes a challenge to distinguish for the regulars at the Fox and Castle. The car park was sturdily fenced off for five days whilst filming took place or the brutal events may well have been terrifyingly convincing as to have an emotional impact on future trade.

Both Morse and Lewis return to The Fox and Castle later in the episode, the extras looking rather familiar.

Morse then drives out of Oxford, down St Giles and out onto the Woodstock Rd, only to surface seconds later virtually back where he started. He passes Oxford student Angie Hartman en route to Worcester College. Although uncomplicated to enter then, the present-day porter was somewhat mystified as the installation of the new star trek lodge was in progress.

Worcester College is a blend of ancient and modern. There has been an institution of learning on the College site since the late thirteenth-century, though Britain's eighteenth and nineteenth century architects created the Library, Chapel, and Dining Hall. The residential accommodation ranges from picturesque 15th-century monks' cottages to modern rooms. The beautiful twenty- six acre gardens and grounds provide a secluded environment with a shady lakeside walk.

As the story continues, Gill and Co Ironmongers reappears as the setting for Sanders place of work and the intrigue unfurls as the delivery of the post at the contemporary offices of Mr. Palmer impels Morse to call on a character at the snooker hall. In the intervening time, Mrs. Crowther is scrutinizing a television appeal, as is the elderly prying Mrs. Jarman.

Mr. Palmer and Jenny are at a hotel on the outskirts of Oxford, as John is spending vigorously at the sports shop. Morse goes to Jennifer Colby's house and becomes acquainted with the literarily garrulous Angie and the somewhat irritated nurse, Mary. The culmination of events being the forerunner to Angie returning to Worcester College and finding Colin Dexter, before she joins Morse at a speech in Hertford College. Gratefully, no one seems to notice it was Worcester College they entered and the main entrance at Hertford College they leave by, a universal practice of utilizing different colleges throughout concurrent scenes to reduce liability in the event of any litigation.

Although John Sanders is under arrest at St Aldates Police Station, it is Worcester College that accommodates a troubled Dr. and Mrs. Crowther who appear to be leisurely meandering alongside the stunning lakeside as they deliberate strategies to exonerate any suspicions in association to murder.

A stressful escapade to discard a suspicious car tyre transpires in peaceful, subdued woods near Caversham, Reading, Berks leads to a surprising interruption causing Morse's chief suspect to collapse with a heart attack. It is in hospital that the early indication of the facts ultimately becomes apparent and Morse fosters a new theory based on a nurse's femininity jealously erupting. With the affair between Bernard and Mary explained, it seems the accidental death is coupled with love and intrigue. Morse and Lewis walk down the hospital corridor fading through the door, quietly Lewis suggests perhaps it is time he bought Morse a drink.

THE GHOST IN THE MACHINE

Aired on the 4th January 1989

Executive Producer Ted Childs

Producer Chris Burt

Director Herbert Wise

Production Designer Ron Stratfold

Location Manager Dennis Firmanger

Writers – Characters Based on a Novel by Colin Dexter. Julian Mitchell

8.

Courtney College is Oriel College, Oxford. The light streams through the windows to rest on animated discussions relating to candidates for the new master. The fellows are choosing between Professor Ullman and Professor Hanbury. Amongst many a phone call, Professor Hanbury becomes agitated, belatedly realizing that the result is a tie, necessitating calling in the visitor.

The scenes change to Hanbury Hall filmed at Wrotham Park, Hertfordshire. Wrotham Park is a Palladian Mansion set in the heart of a two thousand five hundred acre estate seventeen miles from Hyde Park Corner. Designed by Isaac Ware in 1754 and built by Admiral John Byng, the fourth son of Admiral Sir George Byng, it is impressive and despite a fire, has changed little. It remains private property.

An old car pulls away from the gates as a train pulls into Oxford Station. Lady Hanbury, her local landlady and Morse leave the train. Lady Hanbury obligingly offers the landlady, Betty Parker a lift to the Rose and Crown, Harefield Road, Blatchworth, Hertfordshire. John McKendrick drives as Lady Hanbury has lost her license by drink driving.

The next morning sees Georgina playfully escape from her French au pair and race to wake her errant father. Unable to find him as she opens the office door, the office now bereft of the erotic paintings favoured by her father. Lady Hanbury becoming aware of the crime keeps composed, but does insist the au pair should now leave.

Morse is yet again furious at having to investigate stolen paintings of the rich and famous who happen to be on police committees. He is also unimpressed at the photographs of the paintings stolen, but Lewis is savouring the delights of the state of the art computer.

Mrs. Maltby, the housckeeper has her arms elbow deep in plum duff mixture, which Georgina attempts to steal at every given chance, despite warnings flowing from the smiling chubby housekeeper. Unable to help, as it was her afternoon off, she does remember seeing a car arrive as she left. Seemingly, Michelle the au pair was also unable to help, as she had been in Oxford, a friend Roger Meadows bringing her home.

The nursery snuggles contently amongst old toys of a bygone age as Lady Hanbury phones the college to enquire about her husbands' whereabouts.

Moving outside to question John, the gardener, and driver, the scenes change to a Global Retreat, Nuneham Courtney House near Nuneham Courtney, Oxfordshire. Originally owned by Hugh de Courtenay, Earl of Devon in 1310, Oxford University later bought the Estate in 1948. At the time of filming ownership was by the Rothschild group.

Presently occupied by Brahma Kumaris World Spiritual University, it is now a Global Retreat Centre, the aim is to restore balance and focus to life through solitude, silence, and the study of spiritual values. Tucked away in the rolling countryside of Oxfordshire, surrounded by 55 acres of historical gardens and overlooking the river Thames, Nuneham Park, Oxon, is the perfect location to step away from the frantic pace of modern living.

The Church used in the grounds is All Saint's Old Church. Designed by Simon Harcourt, it is unique in both history and architecture. Once a year, the church continues to hold a service.

As Morse and John discuss the story of the well, they move towards the church, stopping to talk with the church behind them.

Delving deeper into the family crypt the macabre cadaver of Sir Julius rests amongst the ancestor's tombs.

Lewis cannot wait for Morse to meet Grayling, the new woman pathologist at the church.

With shared memories of Newcastle, he leads her to the body. Morse has yet to meet her as he is talking to Professor Ullman at Oriel College. Later, after agreeing for Lady Hanbury to leave the premises to visit her sons, he encounters the woman pathologist.

Ullman is not pleased with needing the visitor. The tradition dating back to the religious origins of the college means the visitor is of strict Church of England views. Ullman is a Jew and Hanbury has his own church.

With the church at Nuneham Courtney in the background, Michelle meets with Roger. They discuss keeping apart whilst they wait and with a fond embrace, Roger speeds away in a blue MG.

Morse and Lewis have lunch at the Rose and Crown, Harefield Road, Blatchworth where Morse finds social envy very disagreeable, turning his beer sour and he leaves abruptly.

Returning to Hanbury Hall Morse swerves to miss the rapidity of the approaching MG. The car veers sharply and crashes, killing the driver. Despite wishing to protect Lady Hanbury in his innocence, it transpires that the now missing Michelle was posing for photographs for Sir Julius's erotic collection and Roger was blackmailing him. With Grayling confirming Sir Julius must have fallen from a great height and no blood to been seen, Morse expresses amusement at the 'cunning beggars'. Even though Lady Hanbury's concerns over her sleeping daughter preoccupy her, Morse accuses her of wasting police time making suicide look like murder. Morse delves deeper wanting to know why such a charade was necessary. Insurance money paid on murder, not suicide. Finally allowed to engage in the relished world of computer technology, Lewis discovers a suicide note. Morse is mortified at the spelling and grammar, sure that this was not by Sir Julius. Lady Hanbury was at Nuneham College, Cambridge, and Sir Julius at Courtney College Oxford. (A cryptic clue that identifies the location of Nuneham Courtney a practice that appeals to the team throughout various Morse episodes!)

Michelle is found and willing to give further information. Morse begins to piece together the puzzle. Lady Hanbury had discovered that Michelle was posing for Sir Julius and that Roger was blackmailing him. Lady Hanbury and John had left to see her sons. John drove to the gates and then the banned Lady Hanbury went to visit her sons whilst John fixed the brakes on Roger's car. It seems not only was Roger blackmailing him, but was also going to go to the Sun newspaper, too much for Lady Hanbury to bear. Lady Hanbury had Mrs. Maltby's second-class ticket to London – different timing to her own first-class ticket. Placido Domingo was unable to perform due to illness, despite Lady Hanbury saying she had heard him. Lady Hanbury breaks down and sobs as Morse goes to arrest John. Sir Julius, she explains did not want her, Georgina being adopted. He did want the likes of Michelle, however, even allowing her near his daughter and caring for her. It was more than Lady Hanbury could take so she told John to kill him.

Georgina runs after her mother, fighting off the police. As the police drive Lady Hanbury away, the piercing screams of Georgina pleading for her mummy go unreciprocated. The richness of the magnificent cold stone balustrade encircles the small child desolately hugging a pillar on the spacious steps. The house now a shell and empty of all family connections engulfs the forlorn figure. Yet again abandoned by adult passion, envy, and greed Georgina remains a pitiful orphaned soul crying out with no family to heed her grief.

Morse surveys the heartrending scene and comments on the inheritance Georgina now has.

Also used in Filming

A favourite with film location managers Wrotham Park has featured in Bridget Jones Diary (2001), Gosford Park (2001), Blackadder Back &Forth (1991), The Scarlet Pimpernel (1999),Mad Dogs and Englishmen (1995) and Trail and Retribution VIII (2004), Hammer House of Mystery and Suspense (1984), Lovejoy, the Italian Venus (1990), Mad Dogs and Englishmen (1995),Hart to Hart, Hart and Hounds (1983), Jeeves and Wooster (1991) and Lady Chatterley (1993) to name a few. Framed (2006), Oriel College.

THE LAST ENEMY

Aired on the 11th January 1989

Executive Producer Ted Childs

Producer Chris Burt

Director James Scott

Production Designer Ron Stratfold

Location Manager Martin Lee

Writers – Characters Based on a Novel by Colin Dexter. Peter Buckman

9.

A fishing float idles in the stillness of the canal. The lone angler looks over to the jetty as a youthful couple flounder in the tangled weeds. Shocked revulsion disturbs the tranquility as a headless body drifts in the unruffled waters causing Morse and Lewis to arrive in Thrupp, Oxfordshire and question the landlord of the Boat Inn.

Despite the affliction of a relentless toothache causing Morse to upset everyone from Scotland Yard to his pathologist, the trail of solved murders from London to the University and finally Thrupp return the calm and tranquility to Oxford.

Driving through Thrupp, Morse and Lewis investigate further, stopping – for breakfast of course- at the Boat Inn.

James Scott, the director of the episode joined the rest of the team on the recce and found the locations to be perfect, with no need for any changes.

Amanda Hillwood (who played the part of the pathologist Dr. Grayling Russell) and James went to a nearby hospital prior to filming. Neither had previously encountered a dead body and so they spent the day at the hospital morgue to familiarize themselves with the procedures prior to filming this episode. Filming of the episodes of Morse remained independent as oppose to a series, more reminiscent of a collection of short films. This was in order to promote different writers and producers joining the team and keeping the ideas fresh. James worked with the team on The Last Enemy. The smaller TV productions often proved slightly less demanding on the producers. Major films often use a collection of producers for the larger productions meaning an assortment of different ideas for the team to come into agreement on.

The many film stars appearing in the larger productions are often more challenging. The production of the Last Enemy was exceptionally well organized and the team extremely efficient. The talented actors were a pleasure to work with.

Unable to find answers, the scenes change to place us in Oxford City Centre, with Morse discarding a newspaper in a bin by Carfax towers. From the Carfax Morse goes to watch the croquet at Corpus Christi College, emerging into Brasenose Back Quad.

Richard Foxe founded Corpus Christi in 1517. Bishop Richard Foxe was the Bishop of Winchester and a trusted diplomatic and political adviser to King Henry VII. Bishop Foxe had originally intended to use the College for the training of monks. He then decided that the College should be a place of Renaissance learning for the education of young men in the humanities and the sciences possibly saving the College from dissolving in the Reformation.

Deborah Burns leaves the college peeved at the denial of a research fellowship, whilst the Master is concerned over the disappearance of Kerridge and the impending scandal that could surface.

Kerridge, however, is presently in a taxi at Picadilly, London. He meets Christopher Stone in the Pall Mall club, only to discover an ambiguous request to act for a man he believed to be on a final journey through Greece. Miss Tree is soon to delight Morse as he proceeds from Paddington Station, London to Kerridiges flat in Bayswater, London. Fishing for answers, Morse joins Deborah at the Archery Tavern, London. Lewis, meanwhile, is checking on the suit in Turl Street before helping Dr Russell chose a present. The police station for this episode was Southall TA centre, (now only a small part remains, the rest being flats). Camden Arts Centre provides the location for when Morse and Reese discuss Kerridge.

Tormented by the dentist, Morse accepts a lift from the taxi driver Colin Dexter. In need of relaxation, Morse visits The Three Horse Shoes, Letchworth Heath, Hertfordshire. Relaxation is temporary for Morse as Lewis intrudes on the sojourn. Lewis reveals a callous battering of Kerridge and an addition of Nicolas Battarat to the missing list.

The scenes return to Thrupp and the dredging of the canal reveals missing parts, a church completes the background scenes.

On the trail of the missing man, Morse and Lewis injudiciously hasten to the auspicious corridors of power at Whitehall. The visit to Whitehall soon spreads to the far-reaching ears of Strange who is livid with Morse's tenacity. Severely reprimanded Morse leaves with clear instructions of just who can and cannot bother the authorities. Although Morse and Lewis reputedly visit Westminster in the plot, in reality the filming occurred at the county hall opposite, which is now a hotel.

Lewis soon discards both the drink offered by Drysdale's scout and the possibility of Drysdale being somewhere other than Greece. Following an affair between Ballarrat and Mrs. Drysdale, strained relationships followed for three years later until the death of Mrs. Drysdale. Together with Drysdale's terminal illness, the situation left the possibility of further revelations open.

A scene originally set in writing at the HiLo Cafe in Cowley Road, the story suggesting a permanently stoned Jamaican owns it, was later actually filmed in a former ice-cream parlour in Chalk Farm. Morse and Alex's secretary Carol watch through the willowing smoke screen, as a small child is pitched skywards in rhythm with the colourful reggae music.

The champagne filled aurora of sexual tension is shattered as Alex yields to the shots silently fired a close range. With Brunel University as the pathology laboratory and Hillingdon hospital for the autopsy room, forensic results accumulate rapidly. Furnished with the forensic knowledge of a historical bullet, Morse looks for Deborah at Regent's Park Zoo. Morse intent now on finding Drysdale, not in Greece, but nearer home, returns to Oxford.

A chase ensues across the Cornmarket at Oxford, finally residing in Nuffield Hospital Oxford where Drysdale begins to talk.

The six -page script between Morse and Drysdale involved a dedicated team to bring together the pathos and affiliation of the two men.

Memories for both becoming intense and potent, eloquently expressed the scene illustrates the professionalism required to be part of such an eminent series.

Morse admits that he left Oxford over the unreciprocated love of a woman and Drysdale explains his passion for revenging the demons that haunted his final days. Drysdale did not seek revenge with Kerridge. An escalation of Alex's passion for supremacy led to the obsessive murder of his adversary.

With Graylings birthday to celebrate, Morse and Grayling return to the Three Horseshoes. Sam's arrival heralds Morse offering to buy a drink and as he somberly walks to the bar, the sound of Graylings enthusiasm at the appearance of Sam is for everyone to hear.

Also Used for Filming

Another Country (1984), Brasenose

Lord Peter Wimsey (1987), Corpus Christi College

DECEIVED BY FLIGHT

Aired on the 18 January 1989

Executive Producer Ted Childs

Producer Chris Burt

Directed by Anthony Simmonds

Writer Anthony Minghella

Production Designer Rod Stratfold

Location Manager Dennis Firminger

Writer – Novel Colin Dexter

10.

Students leave Pembroke College as Anthony Donn arrives. Closely observed by a couple from a window across the quad, Anthony retires to his room to arrange a meeting with Morse.

Founded in 1624, Pembroke College is concentrated in its traditional site in the centre of Oxford. The main site, built between the seventeenth and nineteenth centuries with Cotswold stone.

Morse, fresh from heated discussions at a burnt out bookshop in St Anne's Road, Holland Park, London is listening to Kate Donn's radio show from BFBS, Paddington. Anthony's call reminisces bygone days as they arrange to meet in the Botanical Gardens, Oxford. Together they enjoy a somewhat light relief in fish and chips and discussions over Zen Buddhism, one handed clapping and dead men being unable to speak.

Cleverly, a cricket ground is in the background at the Botanical Gardens, although it is not the ground used later in the episode.

All of the cricket scenes were at Mill Hill School. The school occupies a hundred and twenty acre parkland site ten miles from Central London.

As Morse returns to the office to continue to question styles of graffiti, Anthony Donn meets Roly Marshall to play cricket. Anthony later phones Morse, who is unable to answer. Kate Donn, however, breaks radio broadcast to the disgust of her producer to hear of Anthony's death.

Some of the internal scenes are at Oriel and Hertford College, but the majority of the internal shots and some external are at Danesfield House, Buckinghamshire. A large house, Danesfield, at the time of filming renovations was taking place to convert the building into a hotel.

Originally owned by the RAF, Danesfield House changed hands to the Nestle group. Set high in the beautiful Chiltern Hills, Danesfield House Hotel, and Spa overlooks the River Thames and lies between the attractive English towns of Marlow and Henley-on-Thames. Originally built in the Victorian era, 1991 saw the conversion from a country mansion house. Practically desolate, it was ideal for filming – bar the workers. Several days filming had to be around the work at the time.

The team and workers devised a way to work together with the least disruption. Whenever filming was to take place, a bell rang to request the workers to be quiet and again when work could commence. A cozy arrangement, with plenty for the workers to watch whilst they waited to resume the more noisy aspects of their work – the work at this time being plumbing. One story suggests that Morse and Lewis, between shots, would drive in the jag to a local pub.

Filming of Anthony's room and Kate's London apartment were at Danesfield, although purportedly, the Donn's home is at The Old Bakery at Denham, Bucks.

Cranston arrives at Pembroke College, greeted by Roly. He apologizes for affairs of the heart making him late. Roly briefly recognizes Morse as pagan Morse from college days as Kate and Morse walk to The Greyhound Pub, Windsor End Road, Beaconsfield, for a beverage in a teashop!

Morse, disturbed by the events, offers Lewis a swap of a week of decorating for a week undercover playing cricket and masquerading as a college porter. With a dislike of decorating, Lewis readily agrees. It is at the porter's lodge that Lewis begins work as a porter, amongst some hilarity with Morse.

Surprisingly a flashing light Lewis originally sees at Danesfield House appears to be from a window at Pembroke College.

Lewis's interest accumulates in Peter and Phillipa Foster. Phillipa's dizziness in remembering her own phone number puzzles Morse. As Lewis walks across the quad with Roly, Colin Dexter is in the background. With the arrival of Roly's nephew, it seems everyone is ready for cricket. Lewis following Foster in an early call to the cricket ground and sustaining a knock to the head from a shadowy figure wielding a cricket bat, he succumbs to medical treatment.

With the cricket match fast approaching, Morse refuses the company of Kate Donn as inappropriate, but accepts Phillipa's proposal. Despite Kate Donn's apparent jealousy over Morse watching cricket with Phillipa, Lewis is the cricket star of the day. Although Morse sleeping through his brilliant performance results in a dejected Lewis, he continues to come into bowl right arm over and just as he is clean bowled a scream ricochets from the cricket pavilion. Peter Foster is dead. It is time for Phillipa to come clean with Morse and admit they are from Customs and Excise.

Morse fills Lewis in with the story in the toilet, with much amusement at Lewis's reluctance at spelling out his need for the facilities provided. The plot emerges to allow the matches to continue, cumulating at Dover ferry port. Morse becomes aware of the romantic link between Carston and Kate Donn as he supposedly leaves Kate at Beaconsfield station.

Morse then arrests Kate Donn for the murder of her husband and realizing the two deaths is not connected and there are two murders. He accelerates his pace to Dover Ferry Port. Here he realizes the significance of the Hong Kong trips. Morse delivers orders to stop Roly's nephew on the dual carriageway at Beaconsfield.

As realization dawns Morse discovers a deep-seated cache of drugs in Roly's wheelchair.

Also used in Filming

Situated near the Studios, Denham, amongst boasting several famous residents, appears countless times in filming. Midsommer Murders (1997), Brief Encounter (1945), Stairway to Heaven (1946), Rosemary and Thyme (2003), Hamlet (1948), The Great Muppet Caper (1981), A Canterbury Tale (1944), The Thief of Baghdad (1940), Goodbye Mr. Chips (1939) and The Adventures of Colonel Blimp(1943) being a small selection.

Beaconsfield appears in Grange Hill (1979).

THE SECRET OF BAY 5B

Aired on the 25th January 1889

Executive Producer Ted Childs

Producer Chris Burt

Directed by Jim Goddard

Writer Alma Cullen

Production Designer Rod Stratfold

Location Manager Dennis Firminger

Writer – Novel Colin Dexter

11.

A half-naked woman admires herself in the mirror as the phone rings. Her husband begs her not to go, but she accuses him of drinking again. Beside himself, George throws a tape into the river from Magdalen Bridge, Oxford.

Morse is oblivious to the proceedings, mesmerized by the sight of Grayling dancing at the Porchester Hall, Porchester Rd. Bayswater. With oak and walnut paneled walls, crimson drapes and crystal chandeliers, the Porchester Hall is approached by a grand wrought iron and marble staircase and can easily accommodate large parties as in the plot.

New white cord around his neck, Michael Gifford, an architect from Abingdon, lies dead in his BMW at the Westgate car park, Oxford.

Poor Lewis spends the initial scenes at the John Radcliffe hospital having a skull x-ray following a hit on the head whilst prying the secrets of a house found in Sefton Park, West London. He manages to spy a land rover as it drives away, but in unable to identify the driver. Over a drink at The King's Arms, Oxford Morse and Lewis discuss Michael Gifford's diary and the significance of the entry of the name Camilla.

Morse and Lewis then separate and Lewis speaks to Janice at the offices in Highgate, North London, whilst Morse speaks to Brian Pearce at NG scaffolding. Filming for the firm of NG Scaffolding was from the exterior of Jesus College Oxford, undergoing restoration work. It transpires that Brian and Janice had previously enjoyed a short romance, but the happily married Brian nowadays goes ice-skating each Wednesday at the ice rink opposite the Westgate car park. Morse espics a postcard from Michael following a trip to Interlaken.

As Lewis and Morse congregate at Morse's flat, Lewis manages to muster a sardine and radish sandwich from Morse's sparsely stocked kitchen, whilst Morse searches for lost opera tickets. Munching hungrily, Lewis discovers Morse is meeting Camilla that evening in Holland Park, London. Torn from his sandwich as he hurries after Morse they visit the Harrow Leisure Centre, London and confer with Edward Manley about Rosemary Henderson's birthday. Elsewhere at Shepperton Studios car park, not the Westgate, a boy breaks into a BMW.

The freshly painted room echoes the sound of painter's warnings as Janice scampers upstairs. A nervous character, she keeps herself aloof from reality.

Morse and Lewis discuss painting of a different variety with Brian. A fine art collector, Brian's collection of masterpieces provides an eye-catching display. One picture especially catches Morse's attention, as amongst the great works it seems out of place and not by Inchbold as Brian insists.

The burning remains of Michael's letters to Rosemary smolder in the embers of the fire by the cabin in the woods. George Henderson is visibly upset at the betrayal by his wife and seemingly unable to cope without the help of several alcohol-laden tipples. He suffers silently whilst a muted Morse calls on prostitute Camilla, another conquest of the late Michael Gifford. The house was in Holland Park, London, as was Janice's house.

A car thief caught in the Westgate car park swears there were no car keys when he found the body of Michael Gifford as Brian delivers his carefully wrapped art collection to the Magna Gallery, High Street, Oxford. Morse and Lewis meanwhile are at Sefton Park, West London questioning Edward Mannley over birthdays and holidays at Interlaken.

Morse again interrupts Lewis, this time leaving video watching to the other lads. He talks to Morse as they walk down Lime Walk at Christchurch College. Edward Manley has an alibi and Rosemary although admitting to the affair with Michael, also has an alibi.

She was listening to the Archers enjoying a whiskey at what is now a MacDonald's, but at the time was The Carpenter's Arms, Hinksey, Oxford and they find a ticket for the car park. Hoping Grayling can provide some clues from forensic reports, they do discover that George Henderson had liver failure and that the side effects of the drugs for his medical predicament caused impotence. Morse also discovers Grayling lunches at the White Horse. Morse and Lewis travel to see George only to leave following the discovery of Brian Pierces' hanging body, leaving George to phone Edward. Disgruntled with the events of the day, Morse meets Grayling at the White Horse, Oxford.

Unfortunately, the appearance of a rowdy, drunken Janice shortens the social interlude and following Janice, Morse discovers a brown paper bag stuffed with twenty-five thousand pounds.

Driving through Wytham Village, Oxford, Morse, and Lewis return to see George in the woods at Caversham, Near Reading, Berks. They hide from Rosemary's arrival. Based on the characters from Colin Dexter's book, conversion to the TV episode caused some controversy in the village with the suggestion of a recognizable village character having an affair. It went to lawyers before screening, with some small changes made.

Working as a team, with little need for words and explanations, unbeknown to Rosemary they swap car keys. Following Rosemary through Wytham village, they watch her make a phone call and then drive to the library.

George Henderson's body languishes in the woods as Morse and Lewis play out a scenario of tickets changing times that revoke any previous alibis. They go to university boathouse, Oxford (now burnt down), where Edward's alibi has disappeared along with the rest. His keys are unable to open his car further add to the mounting evidence of a conspiracy. He insists that he fought with George and the gun went off accidentally.

As Lewis observes that

"Passion makes a whole lot of mess, doesn't it?"

Edward and Rosemary confront each other at the police station.

With the case finally solved, Morse and Grayling enjoy the delights of a pending Opera whilst listening to Wagner. Missing tickets and replacements again surface, creating a lighter moment where a grin unites them fleetingly.

Also Used in Filming

Frequently used in filming, Ealing has been the setting for over one hundred and fifty locations, notably Star Wars (2002), Casino Royale (1967), Notting Hill (1999), Doctor Who (1963), Monty Python's Flying Circus (1969), Jane Eyre (1996), The Land Girls (1998), The Calendar Girls (2003), The Borrowers (1997), The Hitchhikers Guide to the Galaxy (1981), The Blue Lamp (1950) and Carry on Films.

THE INFERNAL SERPENT

Aired on the 3rd January 1990

Executive Producer Ted Childs

Producer David Lascelles

Directed by John Madden

Writer Alma Cullen

Production Designer Terry Ackland-Snow

Location Manager Charles Hubbard

Writer – Novel Colin Dexter

12.

A torrential barrage of rain batters the colleges at Merton College. The characters now based on the Colin Dexter's Novels, the team shift from the Oxford loving premise to a more sinister portrayal of college life. The discontented colleges depicted in such a derogatory manner, remain so.

Merton College presents a multitude of archways, twists, and passageways that ideally permit all manner of people to stumble across the handiwork of murderers and rogues alike.

It is through these passageways that two men leave the college buildings and venture out into the downpour. Roughly persuaded, a younger male is traveling to the same location. At least the young man, Mick McCoven, arrives at a wall in Ship Street and struggles over, finding himself in Jesus College.

Seconds later, Mathew Copley Barnes, seemingly, discovers Mick throttling Julian Deer at Merton College.

Morse seems frustrated at having to turn his attention from the Oxford Union Debate at the Oxford Union, St. Michael's Street, Oxford, to questions relating to the ownership of umbrellas at the Copley Barnes's home. However, his mood changes as he learns that Julian Deer has died.

Mrs. Blanche Copley Barnes continues to tutor her pianist protégées as the celebrated journalist Sylvie Maxton arrives. Blanche's preoccupation allows Sylvie to reminisce as she saunters through the numerous affluent rooms. Apprehensively, Mathew greets Sylvie cordially as Imogene and her husband Ron join in. It emerges that this is not a social call, but that Sylvie is to write an article on the Master of Oxford College, who had once been Uncle Mathew to her.

No reminiscence for Morse and Lewis as police cordons criss cross Merton's quads, Mick scuttles unnoticed through the labyrinth of archways as Morse speaks to Jake Norrington. Jake discloses that Julian was about to make an announcement at the Oxford Union, whilst Lewis discovers the emptied stomach contents of Spinach, Brie, and Dolcelatte cheese wholemeal quiche splattered in the college grounds.

Congregating at The Barge in Hertford, Folly Island, Hertfordshire, Morse and Lewis discuss their findings so far, before returning to the family photo session at the Copley- Barnes. Here they meet not only the family, but also fabulous Phil, the gardener. The arrival of a ram's skull and horns, neatly parceled, and obligingly delivered disturbs the gathering.

Not the first parcel of such bizarre subject matter, previous packets containing stinking fish and shredding snakeskin's had been anonymously presented.

Sylvie decides to remain unaffected by such events and goes to Imogene and Ron's stables. Enjoying a canter with Ron, she is unaware of Imogene's distress at seeing them together. Sylvie learns how Imogene had had a nervous breakdown. Perturbed about her childhood friend's well being, Sylvie tries to visit her. She is stopped abruptly as the commanding figure obscurely descending from the darkness of the narrow staircase draws level, Sylvie is mesmerized as the heavy jowls of Mathew suggests she withdraws.

Sylvie is not the only one distressed by recent events, but Morse and Lewis having driven around the industrial estate at Folly Island, Hertfordshire, arrive at Park Hospital, Oxford. Here they find some equally disturbing details about Jake and Mick's love life and Sylvie's previous life of crime.

Finding initial tranquility beside the cameo appearance of Colin Dexter and Robert Gasser in the congregation at Oriel College, Sylvie's gaze rests on the chapel window. A chance find by the location team, the window depicts the scene of Adam's temptation at Eve's apple, as the sinful asp entwines the orchard's branches. It is perfect for the story of the Infernal Serpent.

The raging inferno at the house, the chase as Mick is recognized and the austere interview room raise the tempo both visually and audibly. Abruptly, Jake packs his suitcases and flees, a tape tucked snuggly in his socks.

With the inside scenes being Radcliffe Infirmary, the outside being The Park Hospital, Oxford, Morse revisits Mick's mother and is soon in pursuit of her visitor and slowly the facts emerge. As Mrs. McCoven dies, Mick explains he had worked for Soil Scan, a subsidiary of Corby International that has college financial interests. The nineteen eighties had seen a fertilizer reach dizzy financial heights for the company before linked as a cancer- causing agent. Mick had told Julian Deer.

A chain of events unfurl, Blanche spies Amada, the child of fabulous Phil, Sylvie leaves to stay at the Randolph, Lewis discovers where a Three Cheese Quiche can be bought and finds that the fabulous Phil had been there the night Julian died.

Imogene is upset at the stables, but with a great self-assuredness, she is determined in her quest. Morse is concerned and is desperate to find Sylvie, a photo yields the evidence he needs and he walks in to find Mathew battered relentlessly, his lifeless body swathed in his own blood. Rocking, childlike and insecure sits the renowned Sylvie. With reverie, she explains how he had it coming.

As a child scared by the ram's skull in the sand she had screamed, he had put his arms around her, she kept looking at the ram, never him, not once until it was over. Once she had left a green ribbon in his bed and Imo had found it. The fabulous Phil, his daughter, Sylvie could have helped history repeating itself.

A drunken Phil had lunged out at Julian, believing under the umbrella that he was justifying avenge against the rape of his only daughter by killing Mathew, mistaken identity, but not intent. As he was not a member of the elite club when it came to reporting child abuse, what chance did he have?

Imogene pleads with her mother by the organ as Morse and Lewis arrive at University College Chapel, Oxford. Blanche could not of let him live, nor could she live herself any longer. Imogene sways despondently forlorn, she also knew. The two women writhe in guilt as they listen to the quiet insistence of Morse's voice persuading them it is not a matter of guilt, but of responsibility and living.

The choir sings as Morse walks across Merton Quad. Unhurriedly, he turns to Lewis.

"The Infernal Serpent, it was he who stirred up envy and revenge, Milton, Lewis. Paradise Lost".

Morse and Lewis gently fade from view as they stroll through the beautiful maze created by Merton's countless archways.

Also Used for Filming

University College, High Street, Oxford also appears in The Saint (1997) and Mouche (1982).

THE SINS OF THE FATHERS

Aired on the 10th January 1990

Executive Producer Ted Childs

Producer David Lascelles

Directed by Peter Hammond

Writer Jeremy Burham

Production Designer Terry Ackland-Snow

Location Manager Charles Hubbard

Writer – Novel Colin Dexter

13.

The reverberating sound of fingers against a keyboard shatters the silence as Trevor Radford types furiously in the stillness of the Radford Brewery offices.

The smoldering reains of a letter remain unscathed as he secures the safe and hastily descends the rickety old iron staircase. The brewery building seems to ofm seen better days.

Silhouetted against the gloomy recesses, with axe raised, a hooded perpetrator awaits the advancing victim. The proceedings lead to Lewis beckoning Morse with the words -

"You will never believe it, Sir; we have to visit a brewery"

The brewery they do go to visit is not Radfords, but Brakespears, Henley. No longer brewing at this brewery, the site is now a hotel, however after the filming the fermenting barrel carried a sign declaring it to be the one used. This plaque has now gone missing – a mission for Morse perhaps? The choice to use Brakespears was due to it being a traditional family brewery.

(Pictures courtesy of Alan Lister)

Protected against the pungent smell of freshly brewed hops, Morse clutches a handkerchief across his nose. The sight of a man in the fermenting barrel leaving him queasy, Morse quickly moves on to question the secretary and the reasoning behind the burnt letter and carbon paper

The Retail Manager, Alan Lister was Health and Safety officer at the time of filming and conferred with Carlton throughout. Filming began as Henley was preparing for the Regatta. However, the circus was able to park in New Street. As a one way street this did not cause too much disruption.

The brewery is on three levels, the third level being a disused storeroom where a Cooper originally made the barrels. The filming took four days and the brewery was running throughout the filming with the third floor utilized. The noises and suggested smells were for real. The third floor was a storeroom and removing the items and new computer meant the props were able to remain and filming continue throughout. The lighting was sufficient and did not require trawling too many wires across the area, providing good shadows for the plot. However, there was extensive lighting used in the yard. The antiquated safe and typewriter were props. The two bodies were dummies for health and safety reasons, covered with real fermented hops. The murder weapon belonged to the brewery and was a cooper's mallet. It was not a prop.

Outside the Brakespear Brewery, the altered sign read Radfords. A hanging basket that appears by the sign was a permanent arrangement, changed yearly at Christmas and believed to be bad luck if it did not last until the next Christmas

A friend of Alan's had drafted the horses in for the day to add to the affect and the lorry, a TR Bedford came from a museum for the shot.

The boardroom was the brewery's actual boardroom situated on the second floor. For health and safety, the daily checking Carbon Dioxide alarms continued, although at one point, they went off during filming and the scenes retaken. Allegedly, Colin Dexter, the cast and crew all enjoyed the Brakespear real ale. A later programme of favourite shops saw Colin Dexter naming the Brewery Shop as one of his favourites. To honour the filming the brewery commissioned four barrels of beer as a limited edition, the labels chosen to represent the programme with crosswords and jaguars. Delivering the news of her husband's death sees Morse traveling to visit his wife Kate, whilst the radio alerts others to the news.

Farmers Brewery's – McMullen's at Hertford - intention to take over Radfords becomes apparent to Morse and he discusses this and other business details and alibis with the family before joining Lewis for a drink at Ye Olde Fighting Cocks, St Albans. The pub claims to be one of the oldest pubs in England in which Oliver Cromwell is reputed to have stayed.

Situated in the shadow of St. Albans Cathedral it is popular with locals and tourists. Filled with nooks and crannies, parts of the building date back to the 11th Century. It was not until 1599 it was an alehouse. The shape an illustration of the pits used for cock fighting.

One family, complete with children, had arranged to be extras at the Fighting Cocks for the day. Taking their friends along with them, to the delight of the second family, they also became extras on the day. The children joyously put punts brought in for the day to good purpose and both John Thaw and Kevin Whatley chatted leisurely to the young children.

Many of the driving scenes were from the industrial estate that surrounds Folly Island, Hertfordshire. During a lengthy discussion with the Radford family, it seems the brothers rowed before the night of the killing and that Victor Priest would become the manager if Farmer's took over the brewery.

Victor, a keen model railway enthusiast, is with a specially constructed model railway at Magdalen College, Oxford. Although the brothers, Steven, claimed to be in Bristol, he did in fact leave an hour early than first stated. His wife Thelma is bathing in a luxurious pool while explaining her role within the Radford family hierarchy.

Trevor's wife appears close to Steven until his final moments and the elder Mrs. Radford seems rather daunted by the million-pound loan to her son. A referendum concerning the future of the Radford brewery resolves some family issues and creates others. Mrs. Radford arrives in a Bentley now available for hire, previously been seen outside the Radford residence. The large white house that is the Radford residence is High Cannons, Well End, Hertfordshire and the Bentley was on hire from My Lady Weddings.

(Photographs courtesy of Frank & Jacqueline of My Lady's Weddings)

154

The car appeared for filming for two days at High Cannons and one day at Henley, driven home each evening and returning the next day. With an interest in cars, Frank did note that underneath Morse's jag a baking tin strapped in strategic position was to catch oil drips! The actors did drive the car as it was on private property and everyone and the food were as welcoming as always although an enthusiastic Director almost ordered Jacqueline off set, before realizing who she was.

Nelson the solicitor however, visits Victor Priest. The plaque for Nelson's Solicitors reflects images of Oxford architecture. A common practice when filming outside of Oxford, the reflections were superimposed in post editing. Both Morse and Lewis temporarily believe Victor returns the visit in frenzied, desperate attack.

It is by Lewis delving into the history of the Radford Brewery at the records office that Morse finally begins to piece things together. With a little help from Mr. Radstock, he learns how an Ebenezer Knox as well as the original claim by the Radstock family started the brewery. Ebenezer was an Oxford scholar that relished in the thrill of the local prostitutes. In order to avoid scandal he moved to Sunderland with a promise from Radstock to pay him one hundred pounds for each year of his life.

No evidence ever showed he sold his half of the brewery. He settled and married a woman called Priest and started a brewery with Beddows

Morse and Lewis call on Mrs. Priest. The solicitor had been blackmailing the family and Victor had worked to pay him. Victor was Ebenezer's son and the murderer of Trevor and Steven Radstock. Morse remains unsatisfied and feels there is a missing piece. He stops the car in Crossways, near Well End, Hertfordshire, near a small village of Ridge.

As Lewis struggles with his grammatical pronunciations, Morse is enlightened to the post-dated valuation of the brewery at the solicitors. Morse returns to the Radford residence, precisely timed to hear Mrs. Radford tell her husband that she murdered the solicitor.

Also Used in Filming.

Ridge Village is a location for filming in The Avengers (1967), The Saint (1962 /3/6/8), The Protectors (1972), Allo, Allo (1986) and Birds of a Feather (1991). In addition, appearing in films such as The Old Curiosity Shop (1934), Father Dear Father (1972) and Mutiny on the Buses (1972).

Another favourite for filming, High Cannons has also appeared in The Saint (1962, 1963), The Avengers (1965), Randall & Hopkirk Deceased (1968/9), Dangerman, Department S (1969), The Baron (1966), The Protectors (1972/3), and Foyle's War (2002).

DRIVEN TO DISTRACTION.

Aired on the 17th January 1990

Executive Producer Ted Childs

Producer David Lascelles

Directed by Sandy Johnson

Writer Anthony Minghella

Production Designer Terry Ackland-Snow

Location Manager Charles Hubbard

Writer – Novel Colin Dexter

14.

Sweeping views from the Broad Street to the Carfax suggest the location is Oxford.

An impatient Morse is stuck in a queue on the way to a garage. As a girl in the car in front changes cassette, Morse presses on the horn, causing the girl, Jackie, to stall her car. Morse manages to arrive at the garage just in time, but a pregnant Jackie meets a more grisly fate at her flat in Ealing. Awaiting her arrival is a man with black gloves reaching for the masking tape in his glove compartment. A trail of broken eggs and cassette tape lay forlornly outside Jackie's' flat. Jeremy Bonyton calls his wife to say he will be late, as Angie, receives no reply.

Morse arrives at the flat and jokes about what to call a pathologists meeting, only to upset Jackie's boyfriend, Tim. He tells Morse that Jackie was going away for the weekend. Morse having noticed the lingering cigar ends offers Tim a cigar, which he refuses. Having pacified Tim, Morse manages not upsetting Sergeant Maitland just yet. The team get together to discuss the details of the enquiry.

Angie is also discussing the surrounding issues with Boynton. As he draws on his cigar, he reminds Angie of her own smoking habits. Angie in a rather saving grace mode is fearful of what exposure could lead to and so decides to remain silent. Tim also requires the company of Angie to discuss his concerns over Jackie's shopping for a weekend away. He talks to her in a launderette, with Colin Dexter listening intently. Filmed at Elstree, Dot and Pauline seem to be missing.

Morse follows a car from Safeway's at Borehamwood Retail Estate, Theobold Street, Borehamwood, to the TV criminal records office – which is Borehamwood studios, before going to Boyton's garage. The garage is in Watlington Street, Radlett, Herts, although now a block of flats, at the time a false sign suggested Cowley Motors. Amazingly, the filming took two days and yet the continuity of the clock on the garage wall is perfect. It is in this area that the murderer follows his next victim in a Volkswagen. He watches her leave Safeway's car park and drive up Church Street into Old Hatfield.

Lewis is savoring the memories of his wife learning to drive as they visit the driving school – The Transport Research Laboratory Crowthorne, Berkshire. Headington Hill, Oxford lost the parks on both sides and developed an advanced driving school, coming down into Oxford. The scenes where Morse, Lewis and Maitland walk from the garage towards the Oxford Driving School are in Oxford. Later, the scenes on the skidpan are at Crowthorne. Morse is impressed with the school and decides to undertake advanced driving lessons. Morse and Strange do stop for a drink, this time at Kent Pub, Pittshanger Lane, Ealing. However, Morse is off the case, his car starts to go up in smoke, and another woman is murdered.

159

With a connection between cars developing, the interest in the garage becomes central to the investigation. Morse's conviction that Boyton is involved surfaces after their first meeting at Boyton's garage. Morse next visits Tim, whilst Sergeant Maitland calls on Angie. Although Angie is reluctant to talk just then, she does show the sergeant her pot plants at the station later.

The sergeant does now agree with Morse's suspicions about Boyton, although Lewis certainly does not. Scrutiny of Boyton's car by forensics does not detain him. However, it encourages Tim to cover the garage forecourt with foam. In reality, water sprayed the forecourt, the fireman supplying the foam for later shots and clearing the foam away. As a result, Boyton is in hospital overnight. Morse accompanied by Sergeant Maitland breaks all the rules, much to the disgust of Lewis. He is absorbed in trying to link Boyton and car sales to the recent killing and similarities over a space of time. One name does come up – Phillipa Loe. Lewis wades amongst the littered bottles and pizza boxes, his anger spiraling out of control. Morse's obsession with Boyton is also spiraling out of control, although the discovery that Phillipa Loe's assailant is not locked up in prison fuels the fire. As another woman dies, Boyton is safely in hospital and so cannot be guilty. The actor playing Phippa Loe is the wife of Anthony Minghella.

Lewis fears for Morse on his advanced driving lesson with Derek.

In close proximity to the now foam cleared garage a woman pulls up at a house to visit a family member. The quiet street is familiarly quiet as she parks and goes into the house. The ensuing conversation punctuated by social frivolity and companionship, develops into time passing aimlessly. On leaving, an astonishing sight prevails. Hectic events have now transformed the familiar quiet avenue into a crowded extravaganza. A man seems relieved that she is about to leave and informs his colleagues of her intention. Climbing into the driver's seat, she observes the multitude of cameras and sat opposite reading a newspaper in a car, a man's eyes meets hers. It is John Thaw. Realizing she must have held up filming for a considerable while, she leaves rather abruptly.

Derek is indeed chatting about murder to Morse, in a gripping scene the car spins out of control on the skidpan as Derek reaches for the knife in the glove compartment. With Morse unable to stop him, he becomes the next intended victim. With screeching brakes and flying cars, Lewis and Maitland manage to intervene and the knife becomes imbedded in Derek's body rather than Morse's body.

Having hounded Boyton, Morse tries to make amends by offering the wheel of a jaguar special. The day ends with the sound of Oxford bells and the picturesque views of Magdalen Bridge.

Also used in Filming

Radlett is in The Saint (1964), Journey to the Unknown (1968)

The Transport and Road Research Laboratory featured in Into the Blue (1997).

MASONIC MYSTERIES

Aired on the 24th January 1990

Executive Producer Ted Childs

Producer David Lascelles

Directed by Danny Boyle

Writer Julian Mitchell

Production Designer Terry Ackland-Snow

Location Manager Charles Hubbard

Writer – Novel Colin Dexter

15.

Chiswick town hall sees the splendour of the production of The Magic Flute as Morse and Beryl arrive to participate in the recital, Beryl is unhappy at the speed of events. The heavy cloying smell of theatrical make –up hangs heavy in the warm air, as tension mounts in the final dress rehearsal. Colin Dexter is amongst chorus. The Consequences of a phone call to Beryl leave her with little opportunity to voice further complaints about Morse's driving, especially to the non-existent caller. Caught red-handed, Inspector Morse holds the pristine knife. Devoid of any blood, yet perceived as the murder weapon.

Disbelief of the events leads Morse to solicit the advice of Mc Nutt, near Ridge, Hertfordshire. A vagrant interrupts the discussion prior to the discovery of new paintwork to Morse's car. With the Masonic Symbols intact, Morse is breathalyzed and although claiming to be near Maidenhead, he is in fact on a bridge over the M1, near Ridge, Hertfordshire.

Opposite the wonderful St Albans Cathedral, Hertfordshire, the scenes change to an office. Morse, with help from Lewis, uncovers missing millions. Entering a bookshop entrance, they adjourn upstairs to the office. The signs outside the bookshop changed appropriately during the two days of filming as did all phone numbers on the shops nearby. Several other locations used have now changed; these include St Peter's Road and Hill End Hospital, Colney Heath Lane.

The office upstairs also changed from open plan to several rooms and although the offices were empty for the actors, the shop downstairs continued to trade during filming. Unaware of the script, employee's suspicions rose with the request for any books relating to Masonic events. These were then justified on airing. The shop itself was a Christian book- shop and so understandably, was unable to meet the request.

Whilst concealed in the upstairs offices, Lewis discovers computer fraud worthy of Defreyees, in spite of computer records having confirmed he is dead.

Morse cannot resist flirting with Marion, whilst enjoying the views of St Albans Cathedral and Close. On Marion's acceptance to dine with him later, she delights in the thought of a new frock. However, she walks away from the shopping area and into the ancient Roman Verillium, where it would indeed be difficult to purchase any clothing.

Meanwhile, Bottomley is researching Morse's supposed visit to Beryl's flat with haphazardly strewn lingerie, photo's and phone messages; Morse is further implemented and promptly arrested.

The crescendo of music pierces the ears of Lewis and Bottomley as they arrive to search Morse's flat. A specifically built second storey shows Lewis going upstairs to the bathroom. The flat did not have a second floor. The search reveals Mc Nutts body and digging deep into computer records suggests Morse as a perpetrator of domestic violence, hidden by his friendship with Mc Nutt. Lewis searches newspaper archives to discount the implication.

A grateful Morse treats Lewis to a drink at The Royal Oak, Kitters Green, Hertfordshire, before returning home under police guard for his own protection.

Under the composed control of studio settings, Morse relaxes to the calming strains of classical music. Drifting gently to sleep, Morse seems safe from harm and so momentarily, the police protection diminishes. With a dramatic burst flames leap from the cassette and soar wildly out of control, engulfing the sleeping Morse.

Unceremoniously dragged from the raging fire, Morse's paranoia exceeds expectations as accusations abound. To Morse, anyone could be Defreyees and so anyone could be intent on harming him. With tempestuous resolve to flee his tormenting demons, pacified by the familiar voice of his superior, a collected Morse revisits the offices of Marion Brookes.

The information that Marion and Beyrl worked so closely together unsettles Morse. Did they work closely together and on what? Checking the computer records dissolves all evidence as the computer files crumple and seemingly melt into oblivion, reassigning to form the Masonic hand and hammer. With suspicions roused, Morse and Lewis hastily adjourn to Mrs. Brooke's house.

Morse's knowledge of both fine wine and Defreyees signifies a trip to the wine merchant – at Beaconsfield, London Road and to the fictional Chippenham Close found.

Morse is not surprised to find Defreyees and on a journey that ends at the multi-storey car park, at the studios, a frenzied Marion hysterically blames Morse. Although Morse's relief at finding Defreyees distracts from the hurled abuse, Morse's sense of humour returns when surveying Mr. and Mrs. Lewis's reactions as they leave Chiswick Town Hall and the Magic Flute behind.

Also used in Filming

St Albans Cathedral also appeared in Johnny English (2003), First Knight (1995), and Medieval Lives (2004). Whilst St Alban's itself has featured in The Saint, The Man Who Liked Lions, (1966), International Detective, The Conway Case, The Avengers, The Morning After (1968), Randall & Hopkirk Deceased, the Smile Behind the Veil (1968), The Baron, the Man Outside (1966)The New Avengers (1976) and St Alban's Jail is H.M. Prison Slade in Porridge (1974 -1977).

Midsommer Murders currently filming for 2007.

SECOND TIME AROUND

Aired on the 20th February 1991

Executive Producer Ted Childs

Producer David Lascelles

Directed by Adrian Shergold

Writer Daniel Boyle

Production Designer David McHenry

Location Manager Charles Hubbard

Writer – Novel Colin Dexter

16.

The exquisite wisteria covered cottage seems peaceful as a white delivery van winds its way to the door. Mrs. Keeton continues her labour of love as she mixes the aromatic cake ingredients. Humming contentedly at the sumptuous, spotless surroundings Mrs. Keeton is proudly engrossed with her efforts.

Engaged in her quest for perfection, she is oblivious of a man gazing dejectedly through the door. He stops briefly and ponders his intentions, seemingly reconsidering and returning to his car. On the passenger seat headlines bellow a declaration that a police officer is to write a book.

The police officer in question is celebrating retirement in luxury at Luton Hoo.

A photographer from the Luton news was on the set during the shoot in1987, which co-starred Ken Colley, Pat Heywood and Ann Bell.

Morse discovers there is a connection between a missing chapter from the murdered man's memoirs and Morse himself. The staff recalls that the film crew spent two weeks on the estate, with Mansion House doubling as Oxford College buildings and a scene at the Bothy House.

With a few shots also from the surrounding village of Redbourn, Luton Hoo was in the process of transformation into a luxury hotel by Elite Hotels. It was a popular backdrop for major films and TV dramas throughout the 80s and 90s.The palatial mansion is now a private hotel and no longer receives visitors. The prominent architect Robert Adam, built it for the 3rd Earl of Bute in 1767. Little of Adams' work remains, as fire destroyed much of the house in 1843.

Smirke was responsible for rebuilding the house and adding a grand entrance portico. Later still, Mewes and Davis, architects of the Ritz Hotel, added a mansard roof. In 1903, a diamond magnate, Julius Wernher bought the house and decorated the interior in lavish French style complete with a collection of jewelry, paintings, porcelain, and *objects d'art*. There is medieval ivory and jewelry from Spain, rare tapestries, and canvases by Rubens, Titian, Hals, Hobbema, and Fillipino Lippi. There is a Russian collection of court costumes and exquisite Faberge eggs, plus mementoes of the Russian royal family. There is medieval ivory and jewelry from Spain, rare tapestries, and canvases by Rubens, Titian, Hals, Hobbema, and Fillipino Lippi. There is a Russian collection of court costumes and exquisite Faberge eggs, plus mementoes of the Russian Royal family.

The extensive parklands (1053 acres) provide the perfect setting for the house. Capability Brown laid out the grounds in the 18th century, with the modern additions of a rockery.

A little excessive indulgence sees Charlie Hillion sprawled ungainly on the back seat of the car as Mr. and Mrs. Dawson drive him home. Unable to face the haul upstairs, Charlie resides in a lumbering booze- laden pose on the downstairs settee.

As the Dawson's leave, the night closes in and darkness envelopes the idyllic cottage. The silence is abruptly shattered as a gloved hand smashes through the glass door. The shadowy outline of a man creeps into the room and stealthily scours the files of the unfinished manuscript. Interrupted by Charlie, he delivers a fatal blow and leaves with an unfinished chapter intact.

With the creeping light of dawn now descending, Mrs. Keeton discovers the blood-spattered body of Charlie Hillion. Morse and Lewis arrive to find Mr. Dawson there and amongst the investigation. Lewis discovers a young police officer with a more urgent need as he approaches Morse's jaguar. The jaguar wheels originally seen facing outwards have now straightened – without the script revealing any car movement! Following the sergeants advice the police officer is eager to report a brown Renault speeding from the scene. As a moments shyness prevails, it his accompanying officer that enthusiastically informs Morse of the events. With a suggestion of a more increased tempo, Morse makes in obvious he prefers the more methodical approach. Lewis discovers two visitors had been to the cottage the previous day, a Terence Mitchell and Walter Major who is a writer from Evesham.

Transformed by the death of a police officer, much to Strange's delight, the police station is a buzzing hive of activity. Lewis, however, visits the dyslexic Terrance and with a gentle admiration and affection admires his other talents of bird illustrations. Terrance is unable to believe Hillion is dead.

Morse enjoys lunch at the Randolph with Mrs. Dawson, although he is unsure of allowing Dawson to stay in Oxford during the investigations, he does answer Mrs. Dawson's character probing questions about her husband. He believes Dawson is an unhappy man and with Mrs. Dawson thoughtfully nodding in agreement she explains how they were unable to have children.

A pensive Morse walks the sodden pavements. Lewis in jubilant mood eventually retrieves the drenched detective and informs him that they have the killer.

Redpath slouches across the table in the austere interview room. His soft courteous appearance concealed beneath a worried frown. Carefully chosen words respond to the string of questions. A forlorn solitary figure his evading intensity persists and with mounting evidence against him it seems the case is about to be closed. Redpath insisting on insincere explanations and his reluctance for a solicitor does not help his innocence. A livid daughter arrives and then begins hurling accusations at Morse until he wonders how it could be anyone else.

With wrinkled nose, Morse enters the grubby, filthy room that is home to Walter Majors. Unpacked boxes lay strewn amongst chaotically stacked books. Amidst the grime and debris it is difficult to make out the unshaven, greasy haired writer. A cloud of smoke obliterates the ragged clothes sloppily covered with a rapidly maturing dressing gown. The half-closed soiled curtains compete with decomposing newspapers in the aimless struggle of the sunlight to enhance the murky gloom. Walter Majors rests hunched in a small, cleared corner, squashed against a blaring television set. He gleefully proclaims how following Hillion's death he would now acquire the royalties and if optimism could prevail, the death could mean a ten percent raise in the manuscripts retail value. Morse encounters the enigmatic character again, at Hillion's house. With a theatrical finesse worthy of an award, Majors declares a chapter from the book is missing. Reveling in the mislaid chapter, he explains his loathing for the written piece, as it does not tell of glory, but of failure. It is a chapter about a misfortune, a tragedy.

Never solved, the death of a youthful daughter remained seeped in history and the case remained poignantly bare, devoid of any closure. Punishment had escaped Mary Lapsley's killer and justice for her family left a gaping, open wound.

The dank and dismal interview room lacking comfort and leniency dwarfs a troubled Redpath as he whispers in subdued tones

"You know, don't you?

Lewis escorts the fully briefed Dawson to the doorway and as Dawson glimpses the desolate, slumped figure, he flies into an uncontrolled manic rage. Hauled away from the frightened man, he pleads with Morse to interview him. With the clicks and screeches of a protesting tape recorder moaning into action, Morse takes the appalled Lewis to one side.

"She was in the boathouse; a knife was stuck in her...."

Taken to the cells, although Dawson protests his innocence, a burdened Redpath knows he is in trouble. Wilting against the traumatic, nerve-racking events, he leans pitifully against the cell wall. Despondent, dejected and fearful he is unwavering as he deliberately removes his shirt.

The sound of footsteps on the cold, polished corridor reverberates with each step as the police officers strides bring him closer to the locked iron door. A key enters the lock and with a clash of iron against iron, it rotates grindingly, begrudgingly opening the weighty door. Stepping back, the police officer remains motionless as the decelerated fall of the breakfast tray smacks deafeningly onto the unyielding floor. Droplets of hot steaming coffee bounce from the rattling cup as the protracted scampering of the police officer sees him flee the urgent situation.

The Radcliffe Infirmary provides the medical hospitality now required by Redpath, Morse meeting his daughter walks along by Christchurch College. Originally founded by Cardinal Wolsey as Cardinal's College in 1524, Christ Church College took over the site of St. Frideswide's Monastery. The monastery dated back to the earliest days of Oxford as a settlement in the 9th Century AD.

Calling a truce, they talk about the events leading up to Mary's death. Mary had no mother; she had died, meaning the two had become inseparable friends. Her father was at home ill at the time of the murder. Five years persecution followed the implication of her father in Mary's death and so they had changed their names from Brier to Redpath. As they wind their way to The Trout, Colin Dexter makes his cameo appearance.

A diary becomes the focal point of the investigation, originally dismissed as written at varying times and on various typewriters.

Lewis visits neighbour's' of the Mitchell's, before joining Morse at home. In the confined kitchen, an accumulation of a weeks washing up greets him. An old water boiler protrudes annoyingly across the sink and the small drainer is stacked high with dirty pots suggestive of hastily cooked snacks that played little importance in Morse's day- to-day habits. Overpowering the cluttered ramshackle space available, the wall groans under the weight of a generous, well-stocked wine rack. Morse immersed in sparingly given washing up suds, invites Lewis to join him. Cramped together in a kitchen not designed for those with culinary interests, the paint inaudibly peels off the walls as Morse and Lewis vociferously discuss the case.

The Cumberland Nursing Home provides an interesting journey for Morse. The actual location is Shenley Lodge, Hertfordshire.

Meeting Mrs. Lapsley senior, Morse accepts the wizened wisdom of the old woman. Neither he, nor she is fools and so a respect is established. Permission to borrow a photo of Mary and her mum, Morse is intrigued at the label in the jacket, he wonders if this may lead them to Mary's father.

Indeed, it is from an Oxford tailor and Dawson explains where to find the shop. A glum appearance falls on both Morse and Lewis's faces as they find themselves in a wine bar. The wine bar is The Eagle and Child, St Giles, Oxford – renamed as the Shears Wine Bar.

Unable to find the identity of the father from the jacket, Morse visits Mrs. Lapsley to return the photograph.

Mrs. Mitchell is visiting and she scurries away at the sight of Morse. Mrs. Lapsley explains how life has not been easy for Mrs. Mitchell. Her son went to a psychiatric hospital and the father disappeared. The convivial conversation between the two leads to Morse telling Mrs. Lapsley they could not trace the father and Mrs. Lapsley showing Morse a badge from the visit, knowing it was from the father. She also offers postcards of all the visits.

Tracing John Mitchell is difficult as they visit Cowan's and with Morse and Lewis engrossed in volatile arguments finally agree that the five year gap until the appearance of the diary and events that concern the Mitchell's do all coincide. Dawson joins them on a visit to the Mitchell's and again flies into an aggressive rampage. Redpath explains to Morse that he has it all wrong and Morse arrives outside the Mitchell's before the milkman, hoping that the early bird will catch the worm. Terrance is feeding the budgerigars. He admits to Morse that he killed Mary Lapsley, his father found his diaries where he had recalled everything at the time.

Bullied at school because of his dyslexia he had not meant to kill her, but she was laughing and he had a knife in his hand. She was so pretty in clean white clothes, now sullied with blood specks; the blood was on his hands. He had just wanted her not to laugh, not to ridicule. She was so pretty. When his father found the diaries he had changed his jobs so he could watch him during the day and his mother could watch at night, only she would fall asleep. Terrance had been to see Hillion, but his mother did not know.

A tortured Dawson cuts himself shaving as he looks out towards the Martyrs Memorial, from the Randolph Hotel. Morse and Lewis arrive to arrest him for the murder of Mr. John Mitchell. Accusing Dawson of being Mary Lapsley's father, Morse shouts at him to deny it as Mrs. Dawson reels at the disclosure. Dawson admits to being the father and killing John Mitchell and persecuting Redpath.

Within a life souvenir cluttered room, Morse tenderly explains to Mrs. Lapsley. Discussing the details over a game of chess, Morse and Mrs. Lapsley share a silent understanding and finally the ghost of Mary Lapsley is able to rest peacefully, for all of them.

Also used for Filming

The filming of Inspector Morse at the stately home of Luton Hoo was several years before hit movies like Four Weddings and a Funeral (1994), Never Say Never Again (1983), Ellis Island(1987), Princess Karaboo (1993),Enigma (2001), Bleak House (2005), The Wings of a Dove (1997) The Life and Adventures Of Nicholas Nickleby (2001), A Dance to the Music of Time (1997), Oliver Twist (1981),Randall & Hopkirk, Deceased (1991), Here We Go Round the Mulberry Bush (1967) and The Lost Prince (2003).

Shenley Lodge has appeared in The Avengers (1966), The Champions (1967),The Protectors (1973) and A Clockwork Orange (1971).

FAT CHANCE

Aired on the 27th February 1991

Executive Producer Ted Childs

Producer David Lascelles

Directed by Roy Battersby

Writer Alma Cullen

Production Designer David McHenry

Location Manager Charles Hubbard

Writer – Novel Colin Dexter

17.

The sun streams gently through the stained glass window, throwing a soothing luminosity on communion at New College Chapel, Oxford.

The camera pans across the hand painted great west window by Sir Joshua Reynolds, beneath it is Epstein's statue of Lazarus.

Founded in 1379 by William of Wykeham, New College's historic site is located in the centre of the City. It is one of the largest Oxford colleges, with some four hundred undergraduates and nearly two hundred graduates. It is, like all Oxford colleges, an autonomous, self-governing institution. Although the name of the College sometimes seems odd in an institution more than six hundred and twenty years old, its origin is that the College's "official" name - the College of St Mary - is the same as that of Oriel College and so it became known as "the new college of St Mary".

Jeffery Boyd offers the blood of Christ to the small gathering. On the Rebus, an added cross is a special effect, light illuminated. A man rummages in a neighbouring room as a recovering Vikki prepares for her exam. The silence prevails. As a pen rolls slowly from the desk to the floor in the silence, Vikki stands up, grimacing she falls to the floor.

Morse and Lewis rapidly approach New College from Broad Street and down through the narrow, ancient passageways, past the 14th century gateway.

Robin Nye the Head Porter at new College at the time of filming. The team asked Robin to be an extra and during the five days filming, he spent the first day at Westgate Car Park amongst the Lorries, and vans, waiting. Just before the final close of day, Robin, in full uniform, appeared at Nuffield College. The sport's ground at New College also provided much needed space for parking.

Whilst later appearing in the filming at New College, Robin was required to present a speaking part. On asking what he should say, the reply was anything, a tall order for an on the spur actor! It was whilst appearing at New College that Robin noticed a funeral car drive up to await Vikki's body. The funeral director seeing Robin in uniform thought he worked for a funeral parlour. After questioning him accordingly, he was surprised at his mistake and discovering the Head Porter's uniform consists of a suit and hat, the funeral director went away wiser of Oxford traditions. Kevin Whately took a keen interest in the architecture, whilst John Thaw stopped in the middle of filming as the choir began rehearsals. With actors and crew alike waiting, John Thaw stood still to listen to the choir's singing.

The Choir of New College Oxford has gained a worldwide reputation. It is well- known for its stylish performances of Renaissance and Baroque music. The Choir has appeared a number of times at the BBC Proms, and in recent years, it has performed to audiences in Australia, Brazil, Japan, the Low Countries, France, Germany, Poland, and the Czech Republic. The college has not sung masses for the soul of the Founder since the Reformation, but the choir sang at the memorial concert for Princess Diana.

The college remained open during filming, unlike during the filming of Harry Potter. (Robin Nye, now working with the tourists at New College, was also there at the filming Harry Potter.) In fact, the security begin increasingly stringent following fans taking photo's o the filming of Harry potter on their mobile phones and then selling them on e-bay!

With interest aroused by the tourists, Kevin Whately patiently spent time talking about the Inspector Morse series and meeting Robin nine years later he not only remembered his name, but also inquired after his health remembering a concern at the time of filming.

The car arrived on a low loader and a polisher arrived with it, he continued to keep the car spotlessly clean awaiting an appearance. The food again features heavily amongst the memories of the day.

Morse and Lewis question Vikki's associates and learn that Vikki had broken her arm falling from a bicycle the previous week. This had meant a supervised delay until she could take her exams. One plump colleague, Dinah, is bereft with grief as her friend's body leaves the college. Mournfully she retreats from the scene to a hostel for fallen women and gorges herself on ice cream.

With immense sensitivity towards Dinah's predicament, Morse gently questions her. Dinah did not go to the church, as people would stare at her. Morse leaves as Dinah escapes down the rickety fire escape.

Morse and Lewis feeling the need for refreshment visit The Blue Anchor, Fishpool Lane, St. Albans, Hertfordshire

A cheroot smoking Hilary realizes all the files have gone and tries to explain to Lewis how this means all the archives about Pax are now lost. Morse walks through the cloisters with Lance Manderville and Jeffery Boyd cuts the face from a photo of the deceased Vikki and slowly burns it over a candle.

Requesting pathology reports on Vikki, Morse travels to Brunnel Pathology Laboratory, London. It seems that Vikki's body had an excess of naturally occurring substances. Hank, the American scientist is happy to discuss his move to England.

It also appears that a skirmish exists between college and clergy and that Boyd has vanished.

Although not often given credit, Brunnel Laboratories often portrayed the pathology laboratories during filming of Inspector Morse. Many of the cast and crew smoked at that time, with the laboratories being a health and safety risk when combined with smoking an area was set aside in the corridors for that purpose. Breaks taken during filming allowed the members of cast and crew who smoked to disappear into the corridors to indulge. This would leave the set untouched ready for their return. A common student prank would be to sneak into the laboratories, unnoticed.

Once there great hilarity ensued whilst they changed around bottles on the shelves, switched labels and generally made small changes in the continuity of filming. The legacy often remains into transmission.

Morse collects the stories of Vikki's exam papers under her bed and learns that Dinah is missing. Dinah, though, reappears later appears after Lewis questions the owner of a fish and chip van at a lay-by on the A40, near Wheatley.

However, protruding from the top of the van is a shark. This is superimposed, the same shark can now been seen in Oxford, protruding from a house roof, looking as if it had landed from the skies and crashed into the yielding tiles.

Two priests hurry to find Boyd as Morse discovers that Hilary and a Pax candidate Desmond are competing for Boyd's chaplaincy. Vikki had borrowed Hilary's bike, severed brakes meant Vikki had been involved in an accident instead of Hilary. Dinah is obviously upset as she screams down the phone and the ever-irate woman with a dog tries unsuccessfully to speak to Morse.

Oblivious to all of this a man appraises the shapely scantily clad figures circling the sparkling waters of a luxurious swimming pool, a million miles away from the refuge on Napier street that Hilary arrives at.

Morse cannot wait for the legal niceties before bursting in to discover the two priests cleaning the home of Jeffery Boyd, noticeable the wall coverings of newspaper items hollering harlot in bold capital letters. A wall of secrecy closes in around the clergy as they refuse to enlighten anyone any further.

Emma's acceptance of Morse's dinner date suffices in the silence as Lewis struggles to find Hilary's bike among the many at Oxford Station, before collecting his wife from the Think Thin Club Meeting. Horrified, Lewis sees Dinah going to attack the members as they leave.

Morse arrives the next day in a jovial mood. The dejected woman with the dog eventually has her say. Sworn to secrecy since the triumphant awards of the Think Thin Club's Winner of the Year, now everything begins to unfold at Heathmount School, Hertfordshire.

Morse visits Boyd at a church. Jeremy is now unable to answer any questions, locked in his own world. Morse does realize as he and Lewis drive past Shenley Tower, Hertfordshire, that he cannot trust Emma. Lewis explains her son had tonsillitis and Emma was with him, not chaperoning Vikki as she had said. Meanwhile is discussing events with Hilary at Nuffield College.

Founded in 1937, Nuffield College is located in the centre of Oxford. Austen Harrison designed the College buildings and William Morris (Lord Nuffield) a local executive who founded Morris Motors Ltd. originally funded the College.

In the late 1950s additional resources to complete the buildings were provide by the Nuffield Foundation, a separate charity also setup by Lord Nuffield.

Lewis discovers that the Think Thin Club is about to be taken over by Hank Brysdale. Hank had indeed come over from America, the seemingly clever discovery of a metabolic substance being what all slimmers want –a way to loose weight without having to diet. Synchronized swimmers adorn the sumptuousness and lavish preparations at the Think Thin Club as the company ands over to Hank's Health Incorporated Foundation of the U.S.A. With a flurry of activity, Dinah appears with a knife, which Emma retrieves. Dinah had compiled a dossier on the drug Hank sees as harmless and taken the pills and the files to Vikki. Muddled by pain, Vikki had taken the pills thinking they were painkillers and had died. Dinah's revenge and anguish had shown no bounds.

As Emma apologies to Morse, she gently kisses him and says of her intention to resign. She thanks Morse as being known as one of the good people and Morse goes to leave, Irene offers him a drink. He begins to say he has to leave, but Emma pleads as Morse simply agrees to an orange juice. Gently, Emma kisses Morse.

Also Used in Filming

Christchurch College being the location for many a Harry Potter Plot.

New College has also been the location for Harry Potter and the Goblet of Fire (2005) and Tomorrow Never Dies (1997).

WHO KILLED HARRY FIELD?

Aired on the 13th March 1991

Executive Producer Ted Childs

Producer David Lascelles

Directed by Colin Gregg

Writer Geoffrey Case

Production Designer David McHenry

Location Manager Charles Hubbard

Writer – Novel Colin Dexter

18.

The flamboyant character of Harry Field explodes onto the screen. Painting furiously in a studio within the garages of Brockett Hall, the modern art forms spring into life. Colours streak in a riotous display as he frantically conjures images on a plain white canvas. The wild red hair flies unrestrained above the paint splattered old shirt. A flushed face smiles mischievously as he swallows whiskey with lack of any inhibition. The heart and soul of the 1920's and 1930's bond the onset of swing with the rhythms of ragtime and the passions of jazz as 'Ain't Misbehavin' blares across the artist's studio.

The scene leaves the imagination to speculate on his lifestyle as the ansaphone booms out "health, wealth, and happiness". As with many of the Morse episodes, the characters simply leap off the screen, full of life and remarkably rememberable. Immersed in his work and love of life, Harry is oblivious as a car pulls up outside, the driver hesitating shortly before driving off. The tempo rises as an incensed young woman tosses money and a painting at the startled Harry. Temporarily disturbed Harry also leaves abruptly.

Cloaked by the damp nighttime air, a motorbike is thundering along the bleak, spiraling country lanes, near Brockett Hall, Hertfordshire. The tyres yield to the drizzling spray of the dampened roads as the black shadow disappears into the foggy depths of the night, until Harry's body finally rests beneath a viaduct.

In a spiteful revenge, a wife pours acid on a painting of Brockett Hall, hiding the evidence of any connection.

Morse and Lewis examine a dry Harry. His unidentified lifeless remains portray only a bag of keys. It is with a smile that Morse asks Lewis to question the owner of CT's Automobiles. Amused, he observes the owner with a broad Geordie accent explain the keys belong to Harry's motorbike. The collection of Lord Brockett's Ferrari's at Brocket Hall gleaming in the background.

The smiling lips shroud the letterbox greeting Morse at Harry's door. The road name proudly declares it is Keating Road, a play on words. Tom Keating was a famous art forger. The ostentatious, retro style interior provides the stage for Mrs. Helen Field as she enlightens Morse to Harry's need to go away sometimes.

"To drown the demons, darling".

Sipping furiously at the clenched glass's contents, she inhales urgently at the nicotine-laden cigarette. Exhaling, her hand thrashes the air aiding her flourishing description of the colourful lifestyle and personality that was Harry Field.

As Morse returns to the police station, Lewis is discussing the similarities in Harry's paintings with a junior officer. Morse, however, is happier deciphering the joke genealogy. A sideline that provided much of the income for Harry's standard of living. Intrigued by the vivacity of the couple's way of life, Morse meets Helen at Blackwell's Bookshop, Broad Street, Oxford for a lunch hour drink. Amazingly, there seems time to travel to Hertfordshire, as they visit Brockett Hall.

Brocket Hall is now a golf club and the pub that Morse and Helen dine in nestles amongst the green fairway. Close to the main house, it is now L'Auberge Restaurant. The filming was prior to the house being a restaurant and the added props of pub signage and tables of chairs turned it into the public house seen on screen. L'Auberge Restaurant was a former Hunting Lodge dating back to 1760, the building sits alongside the water's edge in its own peaceful environment, overlooking the splendour of the Estate.

Morse is puzzled that the ansaphone message received by Helen from Harry. The message was left four days after forensics say he was dead.

Without any answers, Morse and Lewis ponder the final movements of Harry and the discovery of a motorbike at a nearby pub confirms the vicinity Harry was in just prior to his death. A visit to CT Auto's shows Lord Brockett's splendid collection of Ferraris and the artist studio of Harry Field, would have been found at garages on the estate – these have now been demolished.

Walking from the Crooked Chimney, Hertfordshire, the storm clouds ominously gather. Amongst captivating scenery, an intense mood swathes Morse as he gazes out across golden harvested fields. As the wind blows and thunder echoes distantly, Lewis joins him.

A solitary tree outlined in the horizon still exists, as does the memories of the mood evoked from that scene for anyone returning to the setting and gazing into the distance.

In a pronounced feeling of partnership, Morse and Lewis retire to the Victoria Arms, Marston, Oxford to discuss Lewis's future in traffic. Set against the weakened glow of the sun, the fields stretch into the distance across the hazy river. Morse saddened at the choice Lewis is intent on making, hesitates and questions whether Lewis would be miserable in the traffic division, before agreeing to support him. He watches somberly as Lewis imparts the news to a joyful Val.

With a lead to motorbike ownership, Morse and Lewis visit Lord Brockett's collection of Ferrari's.

It is Harry Field's wake. The event is as large as life and causes raised feelings amongst his many well-wishers. With a thousand pound bar generously left by Harry, the party is in full swing as Morse arrives. Leaving the part of the host to Tony Doyle, Helen whistles the theme tune to Dixon of Dock Green loudly as she agrees.

"It is a fair cop, Gov"

In answer to Morse's questions regarding a Whistler forgery. Morse duly takes the forgery to the Holywell Rooms, Oxford, where an art expert agrees it is indeed false. Lewis, meanwhile, questions the surly Tony Doyle at Nicholas Hawksmoor School, Green Street, Borehamwood, Hertfordshire.

Harry Field senior arrives at Oxford station, much to the delight of Helen. In close comradeship, they discuss events at Caldicote Towers, Hertfordshire and Harry's father leaves to go to the studio. Caldecote Towers is now a ladies private school, which stands in extensive grounds with fine views of the Colne. Lewis is perturbed at the site of an elderly man wandering in. With the knowing smile of a father, the intent creased features smile out above the pink bow tie. The cheerfully suited man surveys the damaged painting of Helen and mutters

"Oh dear, every picture tells a story"

It is unusual for Morse, but the toll of Harry Field finds him reluctant to continue the toasts with a wine merchant. He soberly heads to the College of Arms, London where he discovers the link with the Earl.

Returning to the Crooked Chimney Morse and Lewis, discuss their intuition that other clues must be in the vicinity. Crossing the road, they walk into the beautiful grounds of Brockett Hall, Hertfordshire.

Walking around the corner the full splendour of Brockett Hall eventually reveals more evidence, which inspires both Morse and Lewis to visit the Hall. Brockett Hall dates back to 1760 with over five hundred acres of mature parkland on the banks of the Broadwater.

As quad bikes chase through the undergrowth, Morse's jag speeds up towards the impending meeting with Earl of Brockett Hall. Lewis joins him, stopping at the gates to chat about the beautiful surroundings with an old colleague. An amused Lewis learns he is in luck as the house was for sale at eight point two million pounds. Not a bad profit for a house only used at Christmas and the week before Wimbledon.

Whilst Morse attempts to address the complexity of the Earl's paintings and his questionable business dealings, Lewis is working alone. After recognizing Shenley Towers, Shenley Hospital, Hertfordshire in Harry's paintings, he drives to view the tower. (the tower remains although the hospital is now flats). En route, he encounters Harry's model, Jane Marriot, at 32, Shenley Square, Shenley, Hertfordshire.

Delighted at his detection, Lewis excitedly explains his achievements to Morse, who dutifully goes to visit Jane. A council house, similar to those around, the garden littered with black bags and children's toys spilled onto overgrown grass.

197

Against the grim windows, net curtains flutter in the breeze. Peeling paintwork and exposed plasterwork adorn the walls. Huddled on an uncomfortable sofa sits the single mother, a child cries relentlessly as she draws on a rapidly diminishing cigarette. She had met Tony Doyle at school and started to work as Harry's model.

Having taken in the scenario, Morse meets Tony Doyle at Wadham College. Both Earl and Colin Dexter are also at Wadham.

Meanwhile, Lewis follows Tony Doyle and Mrs. Field from the Modern Arts along Pembroke Street to Pembroke College, Oxford. Morse and Lewis meet up at Christchurch College, Oxford, where they walk from Pepwater Quad to Tom Tower.

It seems Doyle and Helen had an affair. Doyle was loaning money to Harry. A burnt shed at Brockett hall makes Morse wonder if that is how Harry's body was dry when discovered. All questions that accumulate with an eighty thousand pound deposit in Harry's account the week Earl was at Brockett Hall.

As the camera focuses on the security guard, the blare of a horn disturbs the quiet evening. Donning a hat, he makes his way to the car. As he approaches section by section the hall lights up in the background creating a stunning effect. Morse would question the Earl, but the Earl is dead. Instead, he has to speak German to get any further clues and visits Marconi's Warehouse, Hatfield, Hertfordshire, for further explanations.

Conclusions emerge as Helen drunkenly explains her affair and temperamental relationship with Harry. Tony Doyle hurriedly disposes of porn photographs as Morse calls. However, he is able to provide an alibi for the night of Harry's murder for both himself and Helen. Slowly, Morse pieces together the art expert's advice and realizes that Mr. Field senior is the better painter and forger.

Mr. Field senior ecstatically enthuses over his fraudulent dealings with Earl. Bellowing across Christchurch picture gallery, he raises the question of how anyone would know a fake painting, would it not only be if an expert said it was?

Therefore, a bogus painting covered by a sham of shoddy restoration work would only arouse enough interest to say it was a real work of art, a masterpiece – but damaged by faulty restoration. If a painting is never for sale, it never comes under scrutiny. Paul Earl never sold his second art collection; he could not attract the scrutiny. Loaning it to the English Art Collection made him millions but Harry could not allow this. It went against his conscience; he had to clean it up. Paul Earl was not impressed, he had to kill Harry and so Harry senior had to kill Paul Earl.

'Ain't Misbehavin' plays at Harry's studio again as Morse studies the paintings. Jane calls to collect one and explains how Earl did not want the paintings of her, but wanted the model.

Distressed by events of the day, Morse meets Lewis at L'Auberge. Lewis's good spirits soon uplift the remaining moments as he describes how Val feels he would be miserable in traffic, and so he has decided to stay another year. Morse gently smiles.

Also Used in Filming

Brockett Hall was a location for Pride & Prejudice (1995), Willow (1988), Night of the Demon (1957), The Scarlet Pimpernel (1982), Murder with Mirrors (1985), Lady Caroline Lamb (1972), The Stud (1978) and Treasure Hunt (1983).

Christchurch College was a location in Harry Potter and The Sorcerer's Stone (2001), Brideshead Revisited (1981) and The Adventure of English (2002)

Shenley, Borehamwood is close to the studios and so boasts many locations, such as H.G Well's, the invisible Man (1958/9), The Saint (1963/7), Dangerman (1964), The Avengers (1965) The Champions (1967), The Prisoner (1967), Randall & Hopkirk, Deceased (1968), here Come the Double Decker's (1969), The Protectors (1972), Auf Wiedersehen Pet (1983), Alexei Sayle's Stuff (1989), Grange Hill (1991). The films On the Buses (1974) and Man About the House (1974). The Abominable Dr. Phibes (1971) was at Caldecote Towers

GREEKS BEARING GIFTS

Aired on the 20th March 1991

Executive Producer Ted Childs

Producer David Lascelles

Directed by Adrian Shergold

Writer Peter Nichols

Production Designer David McHenry

Location Manager Robert Raynor

Writer – Novel Colin Dexter

19.

The downpour drenches the metallic car roof, as a solitary man ponders over his mobile phone.

Harmonious Greek music fills the night air as Nico's silhouette blends into the dark slatted blinds. He leaves his sentinel and illuminates the dark shadows with a flicker of bright flame. Drawing heavily on his cigarette, he stares intensely at the photos in his hand. Two glasses shimmer in the subdued light; slowly Nico pours the amber Brandy into one and taking the ringing phone off the hook, he relaxes briefly. Within moments, the taxi arrives bearing his visitor. With a fleeting Greek exchange, he closes the meeting and quickly reassuring an elderly Greek woman, he bounds upstairs.

The elderly Greek couple flick through the TV channels, none obviously appealing to the male, he leaves the house to go to the local pub. This leaves the woman to settle and watch the chat show on childless couples, hosted by Friday Reece.

Lewis is impatient for his Greek supper, his wife eager to display her Greek language skills. However, the restaurant seems in turmoil. As Lewis soon discovers the Greek chef, Nico, has not arrived at work that evening. Morse is at Nico's when Lewis arrives, frustrated at the inability of the elderly Greek couple to speak English, he hopes Lewis can help him out following his recent Greek lessons, unfortunately not, but he knows a woman who can.

Unable to question the Greek couple any further they visit The Acropolis restaurant where Morse is able to take out his frustration on the owner.

Morse's interest returns the next day as he contemplates the photographs of a baby, an old wooden ship, a family group, a young woman and a family restaurant in Greece. Unable to make the connection just yet, he looks up to Lewis as the phone rings. Lewis's desk surrounded by children's paintings, frames his questionable stance as he tells Morse that the Chief Super wishes to see him. Morse is in trouble for venting his feelings on the Greek restaurant owner, Valikos.

The reason for his early frustration is about to be solved however, Lewis introduces a Greek interpreter and Morse is finally able to question the elderly Greek couple and ascertain that the baby is the Nico's sisters child.

Evensong streams out from Magdalen College as Morse joins Jerome for a meal. He discovers Randall and Friday are also dining and cheerfully discusses the film Randal made last summer over Greek seamanship, before Randall begrudgingly obeys his celebrity wife's instructions to circulate. Morse is completely unaware of Friday's television fame, but apparently, the couple has the perfect marriage according to the media. As Morse leaves Magdalen College, he passes Colin Dexter in the porter's lodge.

Lewis is aware of Randall's film and has it on video, which he lends to Morse, despite Morse needing to borrow the modern technological equipment in order to view it at home.

Digby Tuckerman collects Maria from Heathrow Airport. Both Maria, and Nico had previously worked for Digby, and it is Nico's funeral. As they arrive at the cemetery at Kensal Green, London, Morse soon leaves in a more amicable mood with Valiakos. Valiakos has an interest in old ship rebuilding, an interest shared by Digby, but whereas they agree on that point, Valiakos is not in agreement with Digby's plan to have such a ship in his latest Theme Park. Morse travels to Tower Hamlets, London, to discuss Digby's interests a little further, with Tower Hamlets Bridge in the background.

The colourful displays and fragrances of Oxford's Covered Market, Oxford appears to charm both Maria and her interpreteur. Maria may have more important concerns than shopping though and it seems she wishes to be alone. She dashes from the covered market into Gold Cross Yard and then out into the Cornmarket. Having lost her interpreteur, she is able to make a phone call, leaving Lewis to explain to Morse that they had lost Maria.

A screaming baby and Greek language leave Morse bewildered and in order to make some sense of the situation he speaks to Deno.

Reluctantly, Deno explains the Maria has no husband and she will not tell anyone who the father of her baby is. Nico knew, it was someone who had been in Greece at the time of the old ships, he was English, and Maria was sure he would marry her, but he was already married. Nico was blackmailing the father of Maria's child.

Chaos erupts as the baby disappears from the elderly Greek couple and a local angler discovers Maria's body, allegedly at the river Wey, Ripley, Surrey. Oblivious, Morse goes to the Oxford Union to listen to a poorly attended lecture by Randall.

Morse and Lewis are at Digby Tuckerman's home, the home used in filming was Highwood Park House, Nan Clarks Lane, Highwood Hill, Barnett, Hertfordshire.

An inebriated Mrs. Tuckerman partially submerged beneath the soothing water of the elegant swimming pool explains how her life with Digby is far from satisfying. Driven to tears by now, she faces Digby's return, as both look horrified by Nico and Maria's death. Drunken and depressed, Mrs. Tuckerman's rage now knows no bounds. She urges Digby explain why despite her previous claims, there was no alibi for Digby. Digby showered in freshly flung alcohol loudly demands a solicitor. In outrage, he vanishes towards the Valiakos home at Chaldbury Manor, Oxford. With knife in hand, he challenges Valiakos and misses.

Morse watching the video of the Greek ships realizes that the answer has been staring him the face all along. Forensics confirms his suspicions and Morse pulls up outside the Reece's home filmed at Huntercoombe Manor, near Maidenhead, Berkshire. As he enters the home, the filming reverts to another part of the house at Charlbury Manor, Cornbury Park Estate,Oxford. He tells Friday he has come for Randall and she whispers that she knows. She turns clutching a small baby in her arms.

With dramatic scenes unfolding, Randall and Friday confront each other as Randall returns from Ship Street, Oxford shopping. The famous, tormented childless couple publically displays heartbreaking sentiment and passion. Emotion rises until Randall quietly tells Friday that she cannot be the baby's mother, not after she has killed the baby's real mother.

Incensed at loosing her domination in life, Friday screeches that if she cannot be the baby's mother then nobody can, it is all within her control. She suspends the baby over the stairwell, determined to regain authority of the situation. Lewis steps in and snatches the infant seconds before Friday plunges over the banister hitting the unyielding floor below.

Morse soberly leans over the staircase and ponders over the almost operatic scenario of the Greek tragedy. He glances at the illuminated figure of Lewis emerging from the shadows below and quotes

"Vigil says, I fear the Greeks, even when they come bearing gifts".

Slowly, he descends the elegant staircase, pausing for a moment to look down and give a thoughtful final glance.

Also Used in Filming

Highwood Park House has been a location in The Saint (1965/6/7), The Baron (1966), Department S (1968),

Jason King (1970) and Jonathan Creek (1999).

PROMISED LAND.

Aired on the 27th March 1991

Executive Producer Ted Childs

Producer David Lascelles

Directed by John Madden

Writer Julian Mitchell

Production Designer David McHenry

Location Manager Charles Hubbard

Writer – Novel Colin Dexter

20.

Morse and Strange remain hidden among the gravestones at Kensal Green Cemetery. The General Cemetery of All Souls, Kensal Green, is one of Britain's oldest public burial grounds. With the famous Anglican chapel and notable personalities buried there. It is the burial place for Isambard Brunnel. It belongs to the charity, The Friends of Kensal Green Cemetery and English Heritage, whose interests are conservation of the parkland and the heritage of the many listed buildings and monuments.

The notable Peter Mathews funeral show is about to begin and Morse is about to journey outside England for the first time. A previous witness, Stone's evidence needs questioning again. Only this can prevent the whole Abingdon gang's release on bail and the work of accomplished lawyers would set murderer of a policeman free. Bernie Walters's presence intrigues Morse, as Stone never mentioned him.

Lewis trudges around the Tilehurst Gazette to discover nothing is missing, with grim determination he joins Morse whose interest in Bernie Walters continues. Perhaps he was working for Larry Nelson. The notorious criminal names involved cause an involuntary shudder. The realization that an imprisoned young man's death from aids would spiral out of all proportion means Morse and Lewis depart for Australia.

An interesting contrast of countries and characters, Morse is instinctively uncomfortable in the Promised Land, whilst Lewis is in euphoric delight as they enter Hereford. Hereford, the fictitious town in the episode, was mostly Canowindra. The Council was involved in making up signs and undertook traffic diversion work to isolate areas from motor vehicle noise while scenes where being shot.

The ghost- like town offers little information initially. Morse and Lewis discover more about Stone, now known as Mike Harding, from the local Royal Hotel.

Mike Harding's mower shop is as deserted as the town. The location for this was an old Motor Vehicle dealership in Canowindra.

Intent of finding Mike they travel to his home, where his daughter informs them neither parent is there. The cottage where the filming took place is now Morse Cottage, Cowra, North Logan Road.

Mike does phone, but refuses to talk to Morse and Morse leaves to find Mrs. Anne Harding. Anne's injured mother leaves the Nursing Home by ambulance. Her ransacked room leaves Anne terrified someone has found out about them. Not pleased to see Morse, she explains that Mike has gone fishing, as he often does and that he will return when he is ready.

Graham Apthorpe from Cowra Shire Council discusses the recollections of Ernie Menday who was involved in the Promised Land Episode:-

"Ernie (now in his 80s) and his wife the late Eva Menday from Cowra were extras in this episode. Ernie, who is a British citizen, came out to Australia after the war. Ernie was a specialist tool- maker during WWII and ended up making parts for the Allies' copy of the Enigma machine. Ernie and Eva spent two days at Canowindra with the filming. They had to join Actors' Equity (Union) before they could work, as did all other extras. Ernie remembers a very nice chat with John Thaw and Kevin Whately. Ernie and Eva had parts in a scene filmed at the Canowindra hospital which was renamed the "Blue Gum Old Folks Home". The nurses in the episode were real nurses from the hospital. Ernie was supposed to be a patient walking past on a walking frame helped by a nurse. They were supposed to be chatting so he said to her "it only hurts when I laugh!"

'Hereford', the Australian town, was a combination of both the towns of Cowra and Canowindra as far as filming different scenes, so for local people watching the episode it was a bit strange with cars driving down one street in one town turning a corner and then appearing in another town instantaneously. Ernie remembers one car being too clean so it had to have a special solution sprayed on it so that appeared dusty.

At the Canowindra Hotel, there was a scene where the locals were watching the Melbourne Cup (horse race) but they had trouble getting extras to participate, as the men were shy. Eventually they were able to convince them and the shot was completed. One of the professional actors was an Irishman (I believe possibly Con O'Neil)he drove to Orange (a neighbouring City) but ran out of petrol on the way back and had to be 'rescued'!"

Mike Harding, alias Kenny Stone, had worked as a stable lad and dreamed of becoming a jockey until the tea jar money went missing. Dejected, his career ventured into the Abingdon Bank raid and subsequently after turning into a super grass, a new life began for him in Australia.

The local police arrive and despite Lewis's delighted interests in the yellow camper van, the police officer Scott questions the young nurse. Morse explains his interest in cattle rearing with the change in the English climate, before Anne and Scott's argument means Morse offer Lewis's services in providing Anne a lift home. Despite Morse's appeal, Anne remains adamant that any new information about the raid would mean a fresh trial.

Morse changes his story to Scott slightly and convinces him he is a private detective trying to establish and inheritance claim regarding the Harding family, also that Anne should have a bodyguard. Lewis takes Anne home- quickly noting a discarded Tilehurst gazette. Both Morse and Lewis retire to their hotel to consider the day's events. In reality, John Thaw stayed at the Cowra Country Gardens Motel on the Grenfell Road and the cast and crew stayed at the Cowra Town House Motel in Kendal Street Cowra.

Lewis arrives with the fresh breeze of morning, as he settles happily to play with the twins. Reading the twins a story, he carefully listens to a phone call and realizes Anne does know where Mike is.

The fresh breeze of morning preempts the blazing heat as Morse in full suit arrives to see the son Dave. Cowra Airport was the location for the fly in scene, where one of the extras was a Council worker. The owner, who is also one of the owners of Belmont, Sheep Station, North of Canowindra, flew the plane. The aeroplane, woolshed and sheep yards all featured in the film also belong to him. It is at these sheep sheds, that Morse is talking to the son, Dave. The sheep station is next to the airfield and the plane simply took off and landed again. John Thaw never actually went in the plane at all.

Lewis remains on guard as Anne visits her mother in hospital, attached to a life support machine, she is gravely ill. This scene was at St George's hospital in the South of Sydney. An actress in a scene with John Thaw was waiting for the crew to set up.

She was in a staff nurses' room familiarizing themselves with the equipment and props prior to filming. She was in costume and make up, but had not met John Thaw. He came in and asked for a tissue, which she gave him without hesitation, since she just had been looking at where everything was. Later, called on set and she was introduced to John as a fellow actor. Briefly, there was a slight confused and embarrassed moment as he had assumed she was a real nurse before. Realizing what had happen, he continued and the scenes took only a couple of takes. However, the actress remembers the cast and crew as all very pleasant, enjoying the small little guest role- and unexpected meeting with John Thaw!

Meanwhile though, Karen's kidnap leads Morse to clash with the police officer Glen, as he tries to tell him what to do. A house, then a banker's residence, was the set for the police station, and its verandah for one of the conversations between Morse and Lewis. The locals estimate 90% of the local population worked as extras during the filming, some appearing on screen, others left on the cutting room floor. However, as agreed by most, a nice way to earn a little extra in time for Christmas, the main filming being around mid May 1991.

Despite the discord between Morse and Glen, the radio alert falls on silent ground as Mike's van lies unattended.

A scene of Morse at a barbeque leaves everyone, but Morse, with a smile. However, Morse and Lewis continue to argue, Morse leaving with Dave who believes he knows where his father is.

Following a picturesque route, for the sake of beautiful scenery as oppose tot ravel directions, Dave takes Morse to Mike's getaway caravan in the bush. The Cowra Shire Council Quarry on Reid's Flat Road was the setting for the murder scene, using one of the Council's Caravans. A dingo slinks away disturbed by Morse and Dave. Morse opens the caravan door, and Mike's gruesome tortured body falls to the dry ground.

Oblivious to everything at this point, Lewis is rather worse for wear having enjoyed a few drinks with Scott. Realizing how things have changes with the rapid events, Anne now admits to Morse that Kenny/ Mike lied at the trial and this means they killed an innocent man. With her daughter, Karen still missing, Anne is happy to help. Peter Mathews may of died an innocent man, but he had made many passes at Anne whilst a young girl. Anne had defied his interest until he became violent towards her. Kenny wanted revenge; Peter Mathews was not driving the getaway car, Larry Nielson's son-in- law was and this had been their insurance. With this, the phone interrupts urgently, Karen urges her mother that the twenty- four hours is up. Morse grabs the phone and says he will bring Kenny Stone to him. Unsure of whom they are dealing with, it is Lewis that recognizes the yellow camper van's driver as Pete Mathew's younger brother Paul. Morse insists on going, he has never jailed an innocent man; it is a matter of pride.

The scene changes to the dramatic 'shoot-out', which were in the now gone Canowindra railway yards. British actor Con O'Neill plays the enraged gunman Paul Matthews with leading Australian actors taking the other roles.

The rising sun and cloudless sky echo the sound of gunshots across the sidings, confusion reigns as Morse tries to speak to Paul Mathews. Anne runs for her child as Scott shoots Paul in the bewilderment. A blood splattered Morse surveys the carnage of the high noon shootings, dismayed he walks away.

Beside the stunning backdrop of Sydney Opera House, Morse awaits the opera's awakening. Lewis placated by the Australian lifestyle awaits the arrival of his wife and the pleasure of a holiday in a land he has grown to love. Leaving Lewis to collect Val from the airport, Morse climbs the stairs and enters the opera's invitation.

DEAD ON TIME

Aired on the 27th March 1991

Executive Producer Ted Childs

Producer David Lascelles

Directed by John Madden

Writer Julian Mitchell

Production Designer David McHenry

Location Manager Charles Hubbard

Writer – Novel Colin Dexter

21.

The outline of a small white van seems insignificant against the grand backdrop of the Fallon's residence. As a solitary bird flutters to the ground in the quiet countryside setting, all seems calm and peaceful. A kindly nurse walks towards the telephone engineer and offers a cup of tea. Family photographs surround the figure of a thoughtful man sat in a wheelchair. With ease, he uses the advance of modern technology to compensate his disability, his intelligent eyes intent on their purpose. Henry Fallon makes a call to his wife, Susan, reassuring her all is well.

In the tranquil countryside setting, both the phone engineer and the nurse leave the worldly wise man to his thoughts. With one cheerful wave back at the window across the beautiful gardens, the nurse cycles down the rural lanes. In jovial mood, she passes Peter on the way to see his father –in – law. Nothing could seem more relaxed and normal in the idyllic setting.

A deafening shot ricochets through the quiet pastoral scene, birds fly alarmed into the azure sky. The flurry of wings rise startled against the sound of their foreboding disquiet, entirely shattering the illusion of the idyllic surroundings. Henry Fallon's blood-spattered, wounded head lies lifeless across the imposing mahogany desk. The vibrant burst of the camera flash attempts to record the gruesome events, however, the faulty equipment means the curtains are withdrawn. Lewis surveys the spectacle as Morse arrives. With a sweeping gaze, the despondent eyes swallow the intimate details. Resting on the framed image of Susan, recognition burns across the lined features. Memories fleetingly invade Morse's thoughts, anguish keenly etched across his face. Painfully, he withdraws his gaze from the photograph and turns to question Peter Fallon on the whereabouts of Henry's wife.

He mumbles agonizingly "Oh, yes, there is a wife, Lewis" in answer to his question and sends Lewis in search of her.

The eccentric brother, William Bryce Morgan, lives on the road to Watlington according to Morse, although Bryce Morgan is actually at Nether Winchendon House, Buckinghamshire.

Nether Winchendon House is a Medieval and Tudor manor house that contains a Great Hall and Dining Room with a fine 16th century frieze and linen fold paneling. It is the former home of Sir Frances Bernard, BT, and the last British Governor of Massachusetts Bay.

The terse Scottish butler and eagerly mounted, unconventional character of a stereotyped equestrian greet Lewis' astonished gaze as he notifies him of his brother-in-laws suicide.

William hurriedly dispatches to inform Susie at the Senate House, University of London.

The cold, grey walls and frosty iron stairway hide Morse as he watches Susie arrive at the police station. As he steps from the shadows to meet Susie, she collapses slowly to the ground. Proffered refreshment and concern surrounds the frail figure as Morse tenderly informs her of her husband's death. Tears glisten in the grief-stricken brown eyes; delicate blonde wisps of hair frame her face as she searches the contours of the familiar face before her. Engaged to Susie in his university days, Morse's desolation at losing her to Henry Fallon had changed the direction of his life.

Morse peruses Susie to discuss informally their lives direction since the daunting parting. Whilst Susie had married Henry and had a daughter and grandson, who died in a car accident, Morse had left Oxford in devastation at Susie's choice and joined the army before joining the police force.

Now known as the Forbury Hotel, Reading Crown Court, Berkshire, provides the setting for the inquest.

Obviously difficult for Morse to listen to the events surrounding the family, the verdict is suicide. On the steps outside the court, Morse asks to meet Susie before she leaves and as Lewis makes a 'bad joke', Morse decides to walk back to the Oxford police station alone with his thoughts. Walking past the arguing figures of a woman and Peter Rhodes, Morse continues deep in thought.

Tying a black bow tie, Morse prepares for a social encounter with Susie, as Lewis arrives unexpectedly. Henry Fallon's doctor wishes to see Morse the next day. For now though, Morse is intent on spending the evening at the Sheldonian Theatre, Oxford with Susie. Lewis is taking his wife to the local Indian restaurant.

"I am a steak and baked spud man myself, but Mrs. Lewis likes to live on the culinary edge".

Hertford College endows the lavish surroundings for the garden party as Morse and Susie try to establish a friendly conversation. It proves challenging leaving Morse to drive Susie home, where with hair swinging in haste she disappears through the front door.

The meeting with Dr Marriot changes the perception of Henry's death from suicide to murder. Such a change leads to a series of questions that places Peter Rhodes central to the investigation.

Heavyhearted, Morse joins Susie for a day at Magdalen College. Together the mood lifts to a spirit of tender, passionate abandonment as they walk through to Addison's walk. Relaxed, laid out on a bench seat, the sound of nature singing gently, Morse is at his most untroubled, gentle side. Susie's laughter and company enthrall him and time seems motionless as they take pleasure in simply being together. Briefly, discussions lead to the car accident and Henry's kindness towards Peter Rhodes.

In jubilant mood, Morse listens to Lewis's update, before joining Susie and her brother for croquet on the lawn. Reminiscent of the case in hand, Morse questions William about Peter. Everything seems to point at Peter being the culprit. As Helen Marriot walks along Oxford High and sees Peter's arrest as headline news, even her meeting Morse at Bray Church, Berkshire to provide Peter with a character reference fails to alter anything.

Subsequent meetings with journalists at the Buckinghamshire Free Press Office reveal the beauty of Helen Marriot. Information that Morse and Lewis ponder over whilst enjoying a drink at The Crown, Bray.

Talking to solicitors, nurses, and William reveal complexities that raise further questions, but it is Lewis that remembers the curtains being closed that sets the trail in other directions. His discovery of an ansaphone tape causes him some deliberation. Wanting to discuss it with Morse, he calls at his flat. A laid table suggests Susie's imminent arrival and so Lewis leaves silently.

As Susie and Morse giggle like school- children, the evening's success leaves Morse in a distant euphoric mood the following day. However, as the day progresses it does see Morse and Lewis chasing in different directions. As the sun streams through the colourful stained glass, Morse vigorously questions Helen Marriot at Bray Church.

Shaming Helen remorsefully, Morse is intent on unearthing the truth behind the car crash. Simultaneously, Lewis discovers Henry's last conversation with Susie transpires to have been with the ansaphone, not Susie. Divided loyalties disturb Lewis's thoughts as he drives to meet Morse. Reunited the detectives realize Peter is not the murderer. However, why frame Peter? As they dispute possible answers, Lewis is saddened at Morse's oblivion that Susie was part of the murder.

Susan talks to Marriott who is telling her she does not have to do this now there is Morse. Susan tells him that she cannot do it, when he finds that she killed her husband it would never work. A miserable man took our child and grandchild from us and had to pay.

A call disturbs their train of thought as Morse and Lewis hurriedly return to William's home.

William stumbles from the house, concern fixed across his features, he is worried that something is wrong with Susie. Morse hastens to Susie's motionless body. By her side is an upturned bottle of pills. Unable to rouse her pale, unconscious body, he lifts her hand gently to his face.

With clenched teeth and steel glaze, Morse clipped voice orders Lewis that he wants Marriot - now. Perturbed at Morse's reactions, Lewis ensures Strange is nearby as Morse thunders into the interview room. Recoiling from the intimidation Dr Marriot does admit his part in events of assisted suicide. Morse's anger and heartache knows no limits. Uncontrolled rage unleashes as he flies for Marriot's throat. With swift action, Strange quickly intervenes and apologizes to Dr. Marriott.

The hushed early morning light bathes the exquisiteness of Magdalen College. In isolation, a distraught Morse leans desolately against worn fencing. Weary and unshaven from desperate searching, Lewis quietly speaks.

Little is said, yet much is understood.

Also Used in Filming

Like many locations, Nether Winchendon has been a location for Midsommer Murders (1997), Oliver Twist (1999), Forever Green (1989) and the Unknown Soldier (1998).(amongst others)

HAPPY FAMILIES.

Aired on the 11th March 1992

Executive Producer Ted Childs

Producer David Lascelles

Directed by Adrian Shergold

Writer Daniel Boyle

Production Designer Maurice Cain

Location Manager Russell Lodge

Writer – Novel Colin Dexter

22.

Set almost entirely at Shiburn Castle, Watlington, Oxford it centres on the Balcome family.

Shirburn castle is now a decrepit, rundown place, no longer open to the public. Lived in at the time of the filming, the true historic story of Shirburn Castle would be worthy of any Morse tale.

It is Emily's birthday, not that she seems impressed with the celebrations. Affection for her friends Margaret and Alfie is not extended to her business minded husband and sons.

Crestfallen at the day's events and family arguments, a weary Emily winds her way through the extravagant castle furnishings to the bedroom.

The grandiose surroundings are unable to lift her somber mood. Brushing her hair, she sighs and climbs into bed. Thirst disturbs her slumber and as she tiptoes her way to the kitchen for refreshment, she finds the now lifeless body of her husband sprawled across the kitchen table. Seemingly unperturbed, Emily wistfully continues with her daily routine, whilst Morse talks to the press. With everyone's whereabouts, established Emily's friend Margaret receives a visit from Morse. She explains that Emily had a child forty years ago, that had died. Margaret is a psychiatrist, presently entrusted with the care of a young girl called Jessica.

Lewis calls to see the solicitor at a house near Hertford Bridge, Oxford before going to Exeter College, Oxford. The reporters are at New College, where Morse briefly chats to Lewis.

A stonemason's hammer is the murder weapon and suspicions begin to rest on Harry, the older brother. It is not long before Harry too is dead, a chisel with the initials SF embedded in his chest. This new evidence takes Morse off the case.

With the press on top of Carfax Tower, Oxford, the view of the drunks admirably played by Danny Boyle and Colin Dexter provide some amusement. Morse is horrified as the press hounds him and mystified by Jessica's visit. With a walk down Turl Street, Oxford, to the solicitors, Morse returns home. Enjoying a wine, book, and classical music he begins to unwind from the tough grind of the day before the flash of a camera disturbs his peace.

It is in Uxbridge Civic Centres underground car park that Morse and Lewis are arguing. Filming was in normal daytime working hours. The actual filming started about 10 o'clock in the morning when the staff's cars were in the car park, and they were on site for about 5 hours, which became a three-minute interlude in the transmission. The fans stopped for filming, but little else was disturbed.

Morse does visit James in time at his office near Chiswick Flyover, London, before shortly after the death of his brother; James also meets an untimely end. He dies whilst he is in the woods with a spade, which prompts Morse to dig up the area.

A skeleton is uncovered, forensic detect stone dust and the body had been brutally bludgeoned to death. The pathologist says the skeleton has been in the ground twenty years, although of course Jessica is not twenty. With the connection between SF and stone masonry, the name Steven Ford emerges. Was this Emily's lover? A trip to Nottingham finds Steven's brother had died a while back and it seems difficult to trace the truth. Morse is becoming more incensed by the press hounding his every move, one in particular, tormenting him over his inability to find the killer and his leisurely book reading and wine drinking pursuits. An unhappy Morse has the case taken from him.

Unable to settle with no case to solve Morse attends the police fete. The joviality is infectious and the sight of Lewis in full costume amuses him. The location for the Family Fun Day scene in "Happy Families" was the North Ealing Leisure Centre, Greenford Road, Ealing. Filmed on the 18th October 1991, the original idea was that Morse, being reluctant to attend this event, was even more humiliated when upon arriving one of the first things he sees is Mr. Punch hitting the Policeman !However, it seems that this intention got lost in the editing.

John Styles was the man behind Punch and Judy and he had the opportunity to have a long chat with John Thaw about his childhood memories and of seeing Punch and Judy in a Park in Manchester.

John met John Thaw and Shelia Hancock a few years later at a charity fund raising dinner. At this meeting, John Thaw discusses John's role in Inspector Morse again and he again seemed interested in the magic show. John Thaw particularly appreciated the magic fooling him, being in good humour. He was extremely courteous and expressed his respect at the effort and the apparent skill involved. It appeared to be an appreciation of one professional admiring another's work.

Morse becomes even further dismayed as the press continue to harass him, but he sees a book written by Emily's friend Margaret. Later, surrounded by press Morse delights in taunting the press to photograph him reading a book and then saying it is where he found the answer. He drags Lewis from the fete and arrests Margaret for the killings of John, Harry and James. SF had been Emily's lover and Margaret's brother. They had had a child together. The atrocious attack and murder by the Balcome men had meant Margaret had vowed revenge. It was easy to deceive Emily that Jessica was her child and form a trusting relationship, worming her way closer and closer to her prey.

A quiet summer's day, in the gentle breeze Emily and Jessica picnic in the sunshine. Mellowing in the sun's rays Emily senses an intimacy with Jessica that only a mother could have. Impulsively, she reaches out wanting to share that special bond with whom she believed was her long lost daughter, Emily mutely wills Jessica to respond, as the silent kettle starts to whistle. Unfaltering in her belief she invites Jessica to share a secret, the secret that she is her mother. Bodies close together she holds Jessica, the boiling kettle screeching in alarm. Within the warm and tender embrace, the torn and tormented child thrusts a knife deep into her mother's heart.

DEATH OF THE SELF

Aired on the 25th March 1992

Executive Producer Ted Childs

Producer Deirdre Keir

Directed by Colin Gregg

Writer Alma Cullen

Production Designer Maurice Cain

Location Manager Cesare Landricina. Italy

Writer – Novel Colin Dexter

23.

The ferocious blaze of the rampant fire signifies the start of a new life. Fanatical activity cumulates in the discovery of a dead girl; stakes protrude from the trunk of a withered tree.

The recently released fraudulent Russell Clark now presides over the illustrious private club. The celebrated opera soloist Nicole Burgess is a member of the exclusive clique. The beginning of a new life signified by burning mementos of the past in a communal fire and symbolically welcoming freedom occupy the small group.

As a young wife lies impaled on a stake within the grounds, the husband absconding to Italy means Morse and a reluctant Lewis have no option but to follow. Unlike the wide expanse and friendliness of Australia that so appealed to Lewis, Italy provides the cultural arts and architecture that fascinate Morse.

In pursuit of resolving the furtive events, Morse seems at home investigating the law-breaking activities of Russell through the cultural regions of Italy. Unbeknown to Morse, Russell acknowledges Morse's presence as he scrutinizes his movements from a side café. Filmed in Vicenza and Verona, the scenery is factual, however, a great part of the filming took place in a specially reconstructed studio set. Accompanying Russell is Mr. Lawrence, the dead girl's husband. Nervous of being with Russell, he hopes he remains unseen.

Russell is unconcerned as he has spoken to a solicitor and Morse's jurisdiction in Italy is limited. However, Morse and Lewis are not as sure as they discuss the case with Atari at the local police station. Atari shows Morse and Lewis around the grounds at the home where the death occurred, he likes Russell despite his past. He even gives seminars to the local police.

The forensic evidence, neatly labeled shows who threw what into the fire, except one number in the series is missing.

After a scorching day Morse and Lewis call into the hotel bar, where the sunburnt Nicole sings, proudly observed by both Morse and Russell. Lewis fetches the drinks for himself and Morse, on his return he is surprised to see that Morse has vanished. Morse apologizes for his hasty retreat the next day as the pair breakfast al fresco. Morse is in rapture, engrossed in the delights of a continental breakfast. Lewis's disgust with breakfast means Morse duly orders another breakfast for Lewis. However, Lewis is decidedly disgruntled with the Italian equivalent of bacon.

Sated with fine cuisine, Morse visits Mr. Haines and reluctant to upset his wife, Judith, Morse and Haines walk in the warm morning air. Haines did know the Lawrence's at Oxford, but he moved to be master at Edinburgh College and had since suffered depression. Morse next visits Mr. Lawrence, who since his wife's death has had to put his house on the market. He is convinced his wife's death was an accident. An American, Patsy, is interested in buying the house. However, Morse sees Russell's girlfriend Maureen and so does not linger, it appears she is homesick, but as for the night in question, all she knows is that Mae Lawrence was having an affair with someone on the course. She believes her husband may have found out. Seeing Russell watching, Maureen passionately embraces Morse, breathtakingly leaving him temporarily lost for words.

With plans in mind, Morse suggests Lewis does some sightseeing and leaves him some leaflets. Lewis urgently tries to run after Morse once he has looked at the leaflets, but in vain. He does see Atari following someone and in turn, Lewis follows Atari, detecting his interest in Lawrence.

Morse's interest is in the exquisite opera soloist Nicole, whom he cascades with admiration and accolades. Wandering through the emerald swathes of trailing leaves, Morse savors the loveliness of his escort as she guides him through the picturesque vineyard, bordered by panoramic views across the valleys of Verona. Nicole is also fond of Russell and she suggested that Andreas should go home. She directs Morse towards a fridge, offering him chilled wine. Opening the fridge door, Nicole swallows hard and says there is no wine. Amongst the wine stacked shelves is a case full of money.

With the conversation dwindling, Morse joins Lewis, who has discovered the handwriting on the leaflets is the same as Mae's, deducing therefore, Mae's lover was Heller.

Morse and Atari unite with temperament fervidly raised. Atari accuses Morse of sensationalizing an affair and a clinical error as Morse suggests incompetence from the Italian police. Atari continues in his indignation, condemning a deemed request to help in a personal vendetta against Russell.

A sympathetic Morse endorses Lewis' solemn promise to his son before allowing the scenic surroundings of Verona's arena to engulf him. With the late sun streaming across his features, eyes closed he relishes the ambience as Nicole prepares to take centre stage. Jolted from his reverie by Nicole's call, Morse bellows for Lewis to stop Hellas.

Striking artwork adorns a priceless manuscript that forms the basis of Morse's visit to Russell and a request to see his client list.

Russell waltzes into Mrs. Haines apartment with murder in mind. Mrs. Haines, who is too weak to take the disturbing dialogue, whispers as Morse arrives

"Alistair did it for me".

Mae too shallow a writer by Oxford standards had ridiculed Mrs. Haines and Mr. Haines held her fully responsible for his wife's illness. Revenge took him to the group that included Mae and his wife, afraid what he would do, killed Mae.

Patsy is waiting for Lewis to join the party, with encouragement from Morse, Lewis display dexterous talents on the dance floor, although Morse's antics leave him with the sorer head.

Morse travels to see Atari, a manuscript of the renaissance is a forgery and the reason Lawrence and Russell are under surveillance. Qaeda, Nicole's husband, is the forger. Lawrence and Russell are about to perform a four and a half million pound classic sting. The difficulty is the finding the authentic manuscript. With Nicole explaining her husband's role, it is difficult to see another accomplice.

A solitary figure remains for questioning, Patsy. Busy partying, Maureen had packed her bags and would help her unpack when she reached America. Unpacking prematurely, Morse recovers the missing manuscript.

With the case resolved, the pleasure of Nicole at the Opera awaits Morse. Lewis asks to go and the duo takes their seat in the impressive arena. The arena vibrates with the emotional chords of Nicole's voice, as an accolade attributes to her talents; the corner of Morse's eye is damp with emotion.

ABSOLUTE CONVICTION

Aired on the 8th April 1992

Executive Producer Ted Childs

Producer Deirdre Keir

Directed by Antonia Bird

Writer John Brown

Production Designer Maurice Cain

Location Manager Russell Lodge

Writer – Novel Colin Dexter

24.

Temper's rise as Alex Bailey's prison door slams shut, the key turns and freedom is fleetingly lost. A typewriter hurls towards the offending door and crashes raucously against the offending barrier. Brusquely presented and softly chastised by Mrs. Stevens, the understanding prison governor, Alex receives a simple caution. H.M.S Prison Grendon Underwood, Buckinghamshire is Farnleigh prison. An enterprising, innovative flagship of the prison service, it currently houses three culprits of the 'Costa Rip-Off'.

The demise of one such notorious villain shortly attracts the attention of Morse and Lewis.

Lawrence visits Wexham Park Hospital, Slough, Berkshire and learns of his need for open- heart surgery. The sudden demise of Lawrence draws Morse and Lewis to the prison. Charlie Bennet is pleased to see Morse the governor is not. The deceased Lawrence Cryer died with his former partner in crime, Brian, leaning over him, a syringe found near the body. Brian has recently been receiving solace from his newly emerged faith. The youthful, bereaved Mrs. Cryer, it seems, has found other ways. Visiting the court room at Reading Crown Court, Reading, Berkshire, the trial for Cryer is held Mrs. Cryer looks suitably upset, ,but her home, the impressive Rossway Park, Hertfordshire shows expenditure that exceeds obvious means and a young admirer.

However, residing beneath umbrellas on a sunny day, Morse and Lewis relax with a drink at The Greyhound, Aldbury, Hertfordshire. A small Country Inn with accommodation and great food, situated in the beautiful tiny, untarnished village of Aldbury. Surrounding a quaint village pond, it provides a perfect setting.

The filming here took three days. Additional umbrellas, railings and seating, transformed the car park to the front. Inside filming only allowed a few of the staff to observe proceedings. One member of staff had a friend that was an avid fan of John Thaw. Clandestinely sneaking her through a labyrinth of unobserved passages, silencing the questions of where she was going, the member of staff smuggled her friend into the bar. Quietly gesticulating to the bar area, the member of staff directed the fan's attention to the man seated there delivering his lines. Unable to believe her eyes, she focused on the man sat almost within touching distance; it was John Thaw. A chair from the bar, used in filming, remains in the hotel corridors.

It is supposedly nearby that Cheetham takes Morse to visit Roland Sheman. Obviously, Cheetham has performed an illegal event that Morse, however, reluctantly agrees to carry out. Leaving Sheman's home, Morse calls Cheetham Lewis as they call for a drink. Lewis is not convinced of Cheetham's fast track talents and is pleased to find he has one piece of information wrong, not all the investors that lost money were ex patriots.

A meeting with Mrs. Bailey at the studio, leaves chocolates to be delivered, however as Morse and Lewis go to visit Mrs. Cryer, Morse sees Bennet in Oriel Square, Oxford.

Believing he should be in the prison and has escaped, Morse chases the frightened man into the Covered Market, Oxford. Lewis meanwhile chases him through the Bear Inn, down Wheatsheaf passage and into the market. A winded, breathless Morse collides with a stall of vegetables and lands amongst the merchandise. Shamefacedly, Morse and Charlie adjourn to the nearby Brown's Café, The Covered Market, Oxford. Morse now has to explain his undiplomatic actions to the prison governor. The Governor and Morse walk around the Radcliffe Camera and down Catte Street, Oxford. Mrs. Stevens's concerns about drugs at the prison seem unfounded, as Lawrence had died of natural causes, despite the syringe found by him. Three syringes in total had gone missing from the prison since her arrival.

Peter Thornton, Brain's son, is covertly enjoying the company of Mrs. Cryer as the Inspector calls. Amazingly, Morse leaves Hertfordshire and Mrs. Cryer's home, drives down Broad Street in Oxford to arrive seconds later at the police station in Harefield, Hertfordshire. Lewis continues to make further enquiries about the investors from a tattooed man whose explanation of his brother being abroad translates as in prison on the Isle of Wight. He has more luck on his next attempt when he finds it is the mother of one of the prison officers. Brian, Cheetham, Morse and Lewis finally meeting up in Slough Nurseries sees the end to a long day.

Morse retires to participate in the choral activities at Eton College, Berkshire with Barrington Pheloug conducting. Morse is singing Bach's St Mathews Passion as Mrs. Steven's edges tearfully into the chapel.

The start of the next day sees Morse and Mrs. Stevens about to go for a drink when they hear Alex Bailey has collapsed and been taken to hospital. Critically ill, Alex has life-threatening levels of dioxin in his blood, co –incidentally, the same drug prescribed for Lawrence Cryer. Cheetham finding a syringe in Thornton's locker calls Morse and Lewis back to the prison. Thornton is adamant he did not do it. The money stolen is in a bank in Liechtenstein, all three had part of the numbers so all three needed to be alive to withdraw money from the account.

Charlie Bennet has a soft spot for Morse and Morse begins to take interest in him by opening old files. Charlie insists Harry Manners murdered his wife, not him. He had served sixteen years for a crime he did not commit. The arresting officer presently imprisoned for corruption increases Morse's interest in the case. The dioxin was in the chocolates from his wife. A prison officer had given the chocolates to Alex. Bennet had ferociously attacked Sheman when he visited the prison, out for character for Charlie.

Charlie had been a chemistry teacher. Morse begins to put the evidence together and with Lewis, drives back past the Greyhound, Aldbury, Hertfordshire. They arrive too late to save Sheman, Sheman is Harry Manners. Seated at the table with the third syringe, is Charlie. Charlie had told Alex about Harry Manners and Alex had laughed at him, so he killed him.

Cryer had surprised him and that death was an accident. Harry manners had killed Charlie's wife, as she would not invest money into one of his schemes.

The episode ends with a buoyant, mischievous Lewis answering Cheetham's questions with fabrication that would be worthy of any novelist.

Also Used in Filming

Recently appearing in Bridget Jones' Diary, the Greyhound, Aldbury and surrounding area has long been a favourite with location mangers. The council has had to stagger applications for filming recently though, the disruption to the village proving harrowing for some residents. The Avengers (1969), The Saint (1968), The Champions (1967), The Dirty Dozen (1967) and The National Lottery Adverts (1994) all filmed in around this area.

CHERUBIM & SERAPHIM

Aired on the 15th April 1992

Executive Producer Ted Childs

Producer Deirdre Keir

Directed by Danny Boyle

Writer Julian Mitchell

Production Designer Maurice Cain

Location Manager Cesare Landricina. Italy

Writer – Novel Colin Dexter

25

The outline of the cement works at Chinnor, Buckinghamshire fades as a tumult of frantic pulsating music permeates through the night air. A juvenile silhouette writhes seductively against the urgent tempo of the hypnotic beat. Green strobe lighting flies of her body as the rhythmic oblivion causes the throng of frenzied bodies to unite in ritual hysteria.

The multitude of spellbound adolescence teenagers start to flow through the open door, creating a fluster of youthful exuberance running untamed over the saturated ground like moths to the dying flame, the horde swarm together around the warmth of a blazing fire.

The contrasting glow of burnished hair intermingles as two girls intertwine. Eyes saddened as a lover leaves with another, the dying embers of the fire dwindle as Marilyn and Vikki leave the crazed scene.

The whispered "it could never be as good as tonight, ever again" lingers on the night air as the scene changes to Harmsworth Park House, Forest Road, Feltham, Greater London and Morse feels the wrath of an elderly lifelong tormenter.

The same tumult of frantic pulsating music pervades the peace and quiet of Lewis and son's revision as Morse drives Joyce home to the playful charms of a familiar youngster. Meanwhile, alongside Pinewood Studios, Black Park, Iver, Buckinghamshire provides the less jovial setting for the youngster's sister.

Tousled haired and sleep filled eyes protrude from the collar of well-worn pyjamas as Morse answers the persistent call of the telephone. The night changes to day as mice run oblivious to their pharmaceutical, anti aging fate in the Brunnel University Laborites and Lewis discusses OSPRE with Strange Lewis later learns that Morse is on leave following the suicide of a friend's daughter and so Lewis is working with Holroyd.

Joyce is plagued with guilt and misunderstandings over the death of her daughter; nothing Morse can say appeases the pain and anguish. He climbs solemnly to Marilyn's bedroom and looks at the cheerful display of brightly painted posters and teddy bears nuzzling together. Geometrical computer generated fractuels and the same frantic pulsating music spread through the room as Morse tries to recall the sorrow and melancholy of adolescence.

Lewis goes to visit the missing Jacko's' family. The journey takes him to Charlie Brown's Garage in Shredding Green, near the Pinewood studio base. Concern over his B.D phenytoin tablets for epilepsy urges his mum to ask Lewis to go looking for the missing lad.

However, Lewis is content to wait a while and meets with Morse at Rickmansworth Masonic School for Girls, Chorleywood Road, Rickmansworth, Hertfordshire.

Lewis does return to Jacko's, another teenager's room with shoes lined up against the wall and the hiss of an out of tune radio playing. The same geometrical posters daub the walls. Jacko, Lewis discovers, goes to a disco in Slough.

Vikki arrives home after a long day at school. Tired, she goes to her room and is incensed to find that her mother is listening to her phone calls. It seems to add to her romantic, exam filled, grief-ridden troubles that impede her life and from which there seems little escape. Similarly, Lewis arrives home after searching a railway line for signs of Jacko, only to find a teenager who looses herself in loud music and reaches solace in areas Lewis simply cannot understand. Horror would perhaps line his face though, if he could see Morse unknowingly entering a school for a sex education lesson back at Rickmansworth School. Lewis preferring to refer to sex, as "you know".

Whilst a promotional tape endorses the uses of the new anti aging wonder drug, Colin Dexter joins the panel. Lewis learns that Jacko has thrown himself in front of a speeding train. Later, it evolves he had swallowed a strange drug prior to his death. With two unexplained teenage suicides, Morse discovers news of a third whilst trying to understand suicide at the Samaritans Borehamwood High Street, Herts.

Morse and Lewis's visit to the Brunnel laborites show a line of blue and yellow bottles, which seem to change in the order of lineup as they speak. They find a strange drug has been located.

Vikki's romantic interest, Charlie, has returned home from a more recent conquest, he listens to Vikki's frantic ansaphone message, but decides to discount the impatience undertones, preferring to listen to a piercing mixture of musical tones. Disenchanted, Vikki's feelings of being misunderstood heighten with her mother's resolve to talk to her. Deciding to relax in the bath, she locks the door, promising to be down for her tea shortly.

As the volume of the music increases, the camera pans drugs concealed in the bathroom cabinet, a razor blade lies blatantly across the bathroom sink.

Vikki's mother calls repeatedly to receive no reply from her daughter. As trepidation mounts, she climbs the stairs and bursts into the bathroom. Hurling back the shower curtain in an intense, nail-biting tradition, her mother disturbs the two small yellow ducks with the impulsive movement. The window is open and Vikki has gone.

Vikki's mother does not help herself when complaining to Morse about her lost daughter. Her views on her daughter's friendship with Marilyn mean she feels the need to question the reputation of the contemporary parenting of Marilyn's family. Whilst Lewis enlightens Morse on computerised fractuels and the effects of butterflies, the pensive Vikki runs into Charlie's arms in an effort to find concord within her tortured existence and Vikki's infuriated mother wrenches the posters from the wall to find a labyrinth of details on local rave meetings. It is enough to send Morse and Lewis to the pub.

The pub is silent, with no other customers and no one serving, it leads to an expressively poignant moment when Morse begins to explain to Lewis the soul-searching reasons for his recent reminiscences. Morse's parents had divorced when he was twelve. His mother had died when he was fifteen years old. This meant leaving Morse to the mercy of his father's newfound love, Gwen.

Gwen strongly disliked the young Morse and Morse had found companionship with her daughter Joyce. Contemplating suicide his vanity even then, rescued him from the depths of depression.

Morse slightly embarrassed at expressing his sentiments, talks to Joyce with Lewis before traveling to the Angel disco and so to the suggestion of contacting the drug squad. Filmed at Elstree studios the disco looks as if it is missing Sharon Watts. However, the questioning seems to unnerve the caretaker, Mike, until he is reassured by the anti aging team. Morse and Lewis have left for a new housing estate near Pinewood studios, where Morse express his disgust at starter homes and struggles to understand youth culture.

Building of the new estate was near Black Park and suggested by a friend of the crew as a location.

As Morse further struggles to understand the significance of an anti aging drugs he becomes mortified to learn that Marilyn had been taking some sort of drugs. Reasoning that he had missed the swinging sixties, Morse further discusses the drug culture and the experiences of drugs in the formative years of Lewis's adolescence. Having requested explanations in an effort to understand, Morse and Lewis hear of an impending rave, where they can collect tickets from an arranged point on the M25.

The rave is underway, filmed at Mentmore Towers, Bedfordshire. Lewis breaks in and with baseball cap in place goes to party and a chase leaves Dr Desmond Collier's car crashing into a tree, a ball of flames engulfing his body. Morse talks to Vikki in order to make any sense of the proceedings and to try to understand Marilyn's feelings. Remaining somewhat baffled, both Morse and Lewis head home.

Lewis stops outside his daughter's room where the now familiar pulsating music continues relentlessly, he learns a friend has given her the music as he quietly utters "Goodnight love".

He retires to his own bed, snuggles up to a book on traffic and stares into space awake, uneasy anxiety creeping across his features.

Also Used in filming

Mentmore Towers also being the location for the Ferro Rocher Advert (1993), The Heinz Tomato Ketchup Advert (1992), The New Batman and the film The Duel of Hearts (1990).

Black Park:- Harry Potter & The Goblet of Fire(2005), Harry Potter and the Sorcerer's Stone (2001) Doctor Who (1963) Blakes 7 (1978) and others.

DEADLY SLUMBER

Aired on the 6th January 1993

Executive Producer Ted Childs

Producer Chris Burt

Directed by Stuart Orme

Writer Daniel Boyle

Production Designer Terry Ackland Snow

Location Manager Russell Lodge

Writer – Novel Colin Dexter

26.

The opening scenes focus on Oxford before changing to the Kings Arms Public House. John Brewster and Jane Folley subsequently leave to walk by the Old School Quad, where John declines the invitation to go to a party.

For the next scene, the camera crew goes to a house near Ascot, Berkshire and the scene is set for the Brewster clinic. Mr. Brewster is leaving for home. When he does not arrive home as expected it raises concern and Doctor Brewster phones the clinic.

With the impending discovery of a body, the venue now changes to the Brewster's house. The house has a garage incapable of viewing from the main window. A fact that later puzzles Morse and becomes a complex part of the scheme. The house selected for this location is at Peppard Common, near Henley on Thames with The Red Lion public house is just visible towards the end of the lane and the illusory phone box makes yet another appearance. It is from the garage that John notices trail of smoke filtering under the doorway. His discovery means Morse and Lewis arrive at Peppard to investigate what the pathologist describes as murder, not suicide. Prior to the fumes surrounding his body, Mr. Brewster had been bound and gagged. The risk of removing the tape suggests breathing equipment to overcome the noxious emissions and so the association of divers later links to both Steppings and Jane. Mark Felsham, Dr. Brewster's doctor closely supports her whilst Morse and Lewis explain her husband was murdered, the first indication that Doctor Brewster is perhaps not as strong as first thought. Dr. Brewster's clarification of Mr. Brewster usual parking habits continue to puzzle Morse as he leaves to question Jane at Oriel College, Oxford.

With John tenuously suggesting an involvement with Michael Steppings, Dr Brewster enlightens   Morse as to the family connections. Morse visits Steppings at Dodd's Water Mill, Chenies, Buckinghamshire.

Steppings is about to visit Avril Steppings at hospital and a link is established with the nurse Wendy. Steppings is without a witness at the time of the murder, he had been at The Black Swan, Chobam, Surrey. Whilst Morse begins to piece together the connections, John is rummaging through Jane's Locker at Longridge Boathouse Hurley, Berkshire, before joining Jane at Oriel College.

Forensic evidence under discussion at the science area is becoming interesting and Morse returns to ponder over the forensic news at home in Ealing. A P.C returns to the Steppings house to discuss security and then discusses the case with Lewis in Latimer, Bucks.

Morse and Lewis then arrive at The Black Swan, Surrey, quite a geographical feat! However, the filming of the series is in sets of three or four and these places are geographically close when viewed as locations in other surrounding storylines.

It takes seconds for Morse to return and visit Nurse Wendy Haslett at 88, St Aldates, Oxford, (opposite Christchurch College) before Steppings is arrested.

Television appeals finally solve the mystery of where Steppings was at the time of the murder. A grateful Steppings invites Morse to Chenies resulting in Steppings offering Morse a cheque, with panoramic views revealed by means of a cherry picker in the river.

Morse and Lewis wander down Magpie Street in central Oxford, discussing proceedings and call at a diving equipment shop in Turl Street. Their journey continues to Longridge Boathouse, Hurley where the discovery of masking tape in Jane's locker points suspicion towards John. It seems that Wendy was about to marry Dr Brewster, although his wife was not aware of it.

With Colin Dexter as the porter at Worcester College, he shows Morse and Lewis to the library – the library being in Christchurch College. John, remaining in at Worcester library, admits to murder. The news is heartbreaking for Dr. Brewster and the supercilious solicitor that arrives to defend John.

It transpires that other hospital stays by Dr. Brewster hold the key. With Jane taken from Oriel Square to the police station, John becomes alarmed at the truth emerging and further evidence surfaces with Morse's visit to Wendy's house. A temporary employment by Wendy as an anesthetist had affected Avril and Steppings life, with the death of Dr. Brewster it becomes clear Wendy was Margaret Jefferies of Harrogate who gave Steppings the alibi at the Black Swan. In fact, she becomes the mastermind of the scenario owing to all consuming envy after Mr. Brewster ended their affair. It seems an incensed Steppings following the unforgivable fate of his daughter presented the catalytic medium and the protective John became the channel to exploit all. Shielding his mother from further tragedy in her vulnerable state, John had confessed to murder. Discussing Wendy's horrendous accomplishments Morse and Lewis drive along the meandering narrow road verging Peppard Common.

Lewis is reading Steppings letter. The discovery of Steppings echoing the demise of Mr. Brewster provokes John admitting to his murder.

Describing Steppings as monstrous, he felt he had had no option. Morse reprimands John over his view of Steppings, questioning how John's father, mother and Wendy had devastated Steppings and broken his daughter in an effort to save money. If he was monstrous, he became so by the events in the Brewster Clinic.

As Morse visits Avril, the scene becomes poignant as a solemn Morse appreciates Avril had also died. Traumatized by the events, Morse discards the roses bought for Avril in the bin. It takes Lewis some restraint not to retrieve them as he mutters over the expense.

Also Used in Filming

The Black Swan formerly was a location for An American Werewolf in London (1981) and Latimer the location for many episodes of Randall & Hopkirk (1968/9) and Department S (1968).

THE DAY OF THE DEVIL

Aired on the 13th January 1993

Executive Producer Ted Childs

Producer Chris Burt

Directed by Steven Whittaker

Writer Daniel Boyle

Production Designer Terry Ackland Snow

Location Manager Russell Lodge

Writer – Novel Colin Dexter

27.

John Barrie is a serial rapist with psychotic and devil worship tendencies. He rapidly transforms from one character to another in an attempt to outwit Morse, following his assisted escape from prison. From Churches to Dark Satanic Mills and Wooded Clearings, the plots vary from kidnapping to Barrie enticing an Oxford Cult by performing the duties of the devils advocate. Nevertheless, the issue remains as to who is the evil spirit bent on retribution. The storyline reaches a pinnacle in a quiet cul-de sac, perhaps a neighbour's house in a suburban area where an ungainly woman complete with stereotyped floral clothing leads Morse into the firing line, all of which takes a psychiatrist to clarify the evil reprisal associated with the devilish spiral of events.

With calculated and rehearsed actions, Barrie escapes from Bullingdon Prison, near Bicester, Oxon. Morse is astounded as unlocked car doors and theatrical make-up help his escape. Together with sleeping pills, all kindly arranged by Dr. Esther Martin, it appears Barrie had evaded any resistance to his plans. His escape raises the danger signals and causes a swift circulation of his description. He relentlessly changes appearance and eludes exposure whilst originally hitch hiking towards Oxford and onto Morse's territory, at times he is blatantly witnessed watching Morse at intimate quarters whilst calling at farmhouses, imparting ultimatums to see his psychiatrist and visiting both pubs and estate agents without any trepidation for detection and incarceration. Stopping for refreshment at a transport café, Barrie calls at The Riverside Transport, Colnbrook Bypass, Colnbrook, Slough. It is also at this bypass where the lorry driver gives the first information of Barrie's whereabouts and nearby is were police stop and search cars and lorries. Given the name Denfield in the script, the area is close to both Denham and Beaconsfield, well- known filming areas for Inspector Morse.

(Photo's courtesy of Andrews Estate Agents, Oxford)

Barrie's immediate need for accommodation takes him to Andrews Estate Agents, Oxford. Now moved, at the time this was in the high street. As Barrie stares at the shapely woman at the photocopier, pictures of the devil disciple's tattoos circulate in the local papers from the Bucks Free Press Offices.

Barrie's delight at Mill Cottage takes the filming from an estate agent to a scenic, picturesque mill, at Mapledurham Mill, Reading, Berkshire. The Eyston Family Estate is an oasis of peace, a natural beauty. Steeped in history and mentioned in the Doomsday Book, it is an ideal setting for a film location.

Whilst Barrie makes his way to settle into the Mill Cottage (the actual mill at Mapledurham), Esther tells Morse of her involvement with Barrie, also filmed at Mapledurham.

Feeling at home, Barrie visits Humphrey Appleton, the storyline requires both a church and a rectory for the scenes. The cast and crew move to Church Street, St Mary's Church, Chesham, Buckinghamshire. St Mary's, is the old parish church of Great Chesham, it stands on a hill overlooking the town. The earliest certain evidence of a church building on the site is part of a Norman window between the North Transept and North Aisle, dating back to the 12th century. The cruciform building is an amalgam of various styles. Notably as Appleton listens to organ music from the church in the vicarage, the lamp is against closed curtains. As he ventures out into the night, the curtains are now open.

Morse discusses Barrie's demands, but a feeling of dread over Barrie's warnings rightly concern Morse. Barrie is now busy visiting and old friend at a local farmhouse, persuading her to join him at Mill Cottage.

Whilst Esther is at Castle Hotel in the plaza suite, Sergeant Brenner becomes involved and Morse becomes more despondent, although Holly does arrive at church and then to the John Radcliffe Hospital, Oxford.

When it becomes necessary to replenish petrol, then the road from Princess Risbrough presents the ideal spot (The petrol station now being a Tesco's Superstore).

The expanding plot increases the location areas. Lewis is next seen visiting an occult shop, which in reality calls for a trip to Princess Risborough. Here Lewis enters modified estate agents and makes both his name and his intentions clear. A ring of fire engulfs a circle of devil worshipers at Burnham Beeches, Buckinghamshire. The dead man is Stephen Trevors. Unfortunately, a second visit by Barrie to Holly results in a shooting and as Holly talks, Morse discovers the real meaning behind the stolen trinkets. Willowbank is not quite so talkative back at Balliol College. Balliol College has an uncertain and chequered history. However, after many additions and changes it was notably in 1973 the first of the traditional all-male colleges to elect a woman as a Fellow and Tutor, and the College has been able to admit women as students since 1979.

An undisclosed, private building in Berkshire granted permission for the filming of the gripping execution and judicious demise of Barrie.

Once contracted the team swiftly leapt into action in priming the location and designing pioneering changes, windows are measured, photographs of the interior and exterior of the house and diagrams are prepared weeks in advance of the preparation for the renovating, theatrical adaptations.

Having unambiguously decided on a thesis of long forgotten decor, shabby dark velvet curtains appeared.

Soon faded, worn furniture arrived. A blue three-piece suite and a dresser were transported for the filming - the blue suite later re appearing in an episode of 'Last Foot in the Grave'. Garden-fresh flowers and images become visible courtesy of props.

On filming, only a lampshade reminded the proprietors of reality. Beyond the interior alterations, the exterior transformed to uncultivated grass. A solitary stone mushroom complements the impression with especially imported weeds protruding from the scattered dusty gravel of the driveway.

Squirreled away occupant furniture remained bestowed in a stationary resident van, as the secreted inhabitants remain in an upstairs room. The intensifying groundwork continues with dense blacking of windows and the erecting of large canvases dimming the brilliance of daylight into a muted, sinister nighttime scene as the car departs on shady and devious errands. The transporters convenient arrival spelt out the trickling influx of white cars, which stickers dynamically converted into police cars. Barrie's car and Morse's jag arriving by the same method. As the gleaming, polished jaguar remained silently redundant on the margins, so too in the adjoining coach lingered the impeccably laundered, uncomplaining extras, all resolutely residing in a subdued manner to discover they were also superfluous.

A purpose built tunnel by the garage transformed scenes of Barrie in his car as nighttime, not the daylight hours used in filming.

In the throes of filming, Barrie as a significantly different character of a graceless, lumbering, clumsy woman in a floral dress comes into view. The actor Keith Allen (Voted the 47th sexiest male in Wales, 2006!) had two dresses, one without bloodstains, and one with bloodstains. The owners of the house watching Keith Allen get ready for the scene warned him that the sunlight through the dress made it noticeably transparent and Keith Allen replied

"do you mind, these cost £19.99 each from C & A's."

An unrehearsed stumble followed as he tottered fearfully on high heels to the doorway.

The stipulated scenes where he was devouring a freshly made sandwich in essence demanded a new sandwich for each take meaning employing a sum of two additional loaves for this one shot, with one man heavily engaged in making further supplementary sandwiches until the perfectly executed routine was accepted. In the scenes with dialogues between two or more performers, the actors had to replicate each speech as the camera shot the exchange from different angles. The representation of a shooting necessitated numerous attempts to guarantee the smoldering impression of the gunshot was precisely correct, triggering an extra day of filming. Vigilant camouflage hid the fact the weather conditions had drastically changed in the variation of the day's filming of this section and the connecting parts retaken for perfection involved a great deal of preplanning and innovative technology. This then lead to the filming in the garage not being completed on time and having to be conducted later at the studio in a replica of the garage used. Inevitably photographing every element and featured aspect in order to reproduce it precisely, it even incorporated borrowing the stockpiled family's guinea pig food in justification of someone perceiving any changes!

In contemplating several houses within the area, it transpired that this individual residence proffered a substantial car park nearby and the quiet, dusty lane leading to the house. The car park was capable of being utilized by an entire entourage, from minders to extras, caravans to burger vans with the neighbour's being encouraged to join the crew for mealtimes. The period of filming regularly accumulated with the neighbour's communally watching the experience and jointly partying in the street.

It later emerged that diagonally across the street two young girls watched from the windows, speedily concealed accordingly. Shortly afterwards it transpires that two inconsequential minors, completely oblivious of the filming, allegedly scuttled homewards, alerting their mothers of an impending siege in the region.

Approximately six minutes revealed in airing, reputedly at an expense up to two million pounds for the fleeting installment was calculated and consuming, but effectual. However, apparently, Kevin Whately would contentedly sit and read the newspapers (namely the Sun, it is rumoured), whilst waiting for each successive scene for his character, not too intimidating an experience for the practiced artist. When all was completed, the driveway previously swathed with artificial blood lingered for several days, the only indicator that the throng of crew and associates had ever swarmed the area, their existence obliterated and condensed into unforgettable reminders of a barely credible encounter.

Esther had first met Barrie ten years ago. Broken down on her motorbike, Barrie, Trevor and Holly stopped to help, but the men raped her. She saw the tattoo and years later following his arrest, she recognized him. Not expecting Morse to understand, she suggests when he finds the owner of the ring, another victim, he should look into her eyes and find his answers there.

Also used in filming

Mapledurham was used in The Eagle has Landed (1976). (2001), Dr Who (1963) and Blake's 7(1978).

Burnham Beeches is again an area frequently used in filming, notable in Robin Hood, Prince of Thieves (1991), Doctor Who (1963), Goldfinger (1964),The Crying Game (1992), Gulliver's Travels (1996), The Wind in the Willows (1996), Carry on Camping (1976), Carry on Behind(1975), Carry on England(1976) and A Town like Alice (1956) .

TWILIGHT OF THE GODS

Aired on the 20th January 1993

Executive Producer Ted Childs

Producer Chris Burt

Directed by Herbert Wise

Writer Julian Mitchell

Production Designer Terry Ackland Snow

Location Manager Russell Lodge

Writer – Novel Colin Dexter

28.

The tensions of a Welsh Diva vibrate through the agreeable surroundings of Holywell Music Room. Robert Gasser listens, enthralled by the intensity of her performance. Gladys chastises a soloist for her unemotional recital, the girl being chastised actually providing the voice for Gladys in the episode. A standing ovation for Gladys contrasts with the repellent scenes of the corpse of Nevillle Grimshaw languishing in a canoe at the River Wey, Newark Priory, Ripley, Surrey.

With close admiration by her entourage, Gladys is at Englefield House, Berkshire where she reveals her true personality.

A great degree of this episode is set in the magnificent surroundings of Englefield House, Berkshire. Englefield Estate is a comparatively new addition to the location mangers repertoire following camaraderie between Robert Gasser from the Oxford Colleges and the Benyon Family whose home is at Englefield. Built in the Tudor period, the house underwent substantial additions and alterations in the 18th and 19th centuries. The Englefield Estate covers some 14,000 acres in Berkshire and North Hampshire. It consists of farmland, forestry, residential and commercial property. Over 1000 people rely on the Estate for their livelihood or for their housing needs.

The transformation of the home of the Benyon family as filming commences sees the grand hallway becoming unrecognizable as the office as desks and office equipment fill the empty corridors.

The library provides the piano for later scenes, whilst Baydon's office looses its magnificent dinning table and again office furniture becomes a replacement. Only furniture moved for the filming, items such as pictures all had to remain firmly in place.

(Englefield Estate kindly provided the Photographs)

Scenes in the grounds around the Englefield estate provided a helicopter-landing site. The noise was apparently constant and deafening during the filming for the residents of the Estate and the gardener recalls the heads of the newly planted flowers lost in the wind.

As Morse buys roses for Gladys's evening performance, the journalist Neville's last moments unfold. He had apparently being staying at the Randolph and writing about Baydon.

The preparations for the Encaenia continue amongst the flurry of heated phone calls attributing to the temperamental character of Baydon.

As the procession flows through Broad Street, Oxford to the Sheldonian and The Schools Quad, the brutal shooting of the infamous vocalist again attracts more attention.

Filming for the full scene was on a Sunday, a few extras used, but enough people gathered to watch the filming to portray the correct ambience.

In reality, the parade goes from Brasenose to Hertford College. However, although discussed as the route taken, the actual route shown was the parade going down Broad Street.

A nervous Strange allows Morse to investigate and the focus is on Tom's Quad, Christchurch and Oriel College for the interrogation of the suspects. An agitated Chancellor, with Colin Dexter behind him, enlists the help of the Welsh Vice Chancellor. With the suspects becoming hungry, Morse and a hungry Lewis drive through Denham Village, Bucks, nobody stopping to eat as Morse ploughs on. The Chancellors becoming irate at the police investigation, which he feels, the proctors should be conducting. Lewis becomes a little 'Huffy Puffy' at Englefield as a ransacked daughter's room suggests links to Baydon's past. As Gladys languishes close to death in I.C.U. at the John Radcliffe 2 Hospital, Oxford, two units of blood try to replace the lost fluids. As one bag remains unlabelled, perhaps there is a sinister plot to put Gladys in further danger! However, an expectant sister returns to stage a bedside vigil.

The Bodleian Library, Oxford becomes the site for the discovery of the murder weapon, which ultimately leads to the discovery of Baydon's Nazi past and a poor shot. Confessions from a tortured Jewish student lead Morse and Lewis back to Englefield House. Baydon's continued persecution in attempt to hide his past now involved a vicar murdering his son at is request, whilst the Eastern European student had attempted to shoot Baydon. Caught in the crossfire, Gladys lays in the hospital bed. With blurred vision, Gladys moistens dry lips and smiles at Marrie.

A flower laden dressing room lies unattended, the heady aroma lies in the air as the crescendo of operatic music rests on the wilted roses bought earlier in the day by Morse. At the end of a harrowing day, the murder now solved, Morse drives past the Holywell Rooms. As he drives past his window is open, as he looks out of the window it is closed and then open again as he drives off! A few words of cancellation on a poster are scarcely able to portray the dreadful events of the day.

Also Used in Filming

Englefield House featured in a Woman of Substance (1984), Jeeves and Wooster (1991), MacGyver: Lost Treasure of Atlantis (1993), The Haunting of Helen Walker, a.k.a. The Turn of the Screw (1995) and Charlotte Gray (2001).

THE WAY THROUGH THE WOODS

Aired on the 28th November 1995

Executive Producer Ted Childs

Producer Chris Burt

Directed by John Madden

Writer Russell Lewis

Production Designer Maria Djurkovic

Location Manager Russell Lodge

Writer – Novel Colin Dexter

29.

The opening scenes fluctuate between Oxford Prison (now a malmaison hotel), a man walking a dog in Leith Hill, Surrey and the affluent grounds of Exeter College.

The sound of the woodpecker's shrill call drifts through the breeze at Leith Hill, Surrey. A skull rolls down the undulating pathway in the woods, chased by a playful dog. It rests hidden in the undergrowth. The musical climax against the Radcliffe Camera contrasts with the stark reality of the murder of Steven Parnell and the whispered "not the last, not the girl. Morse weaves his way past the press release over Parnell and contends with Johnson and Lewis being on active duty whilst he remains on clerical work.

George Daley is at home with his wife and son. On hearing of the death on the radio, he goes to fill his car with petrol. Whilst George Daley drives to Blenhiem, Morse decides to renew a recent acquaintance with Clare Osbourne at Thornton's Bookshop in Turl Street, Oxford – now Past Times. In fact, during filming, John Thaw would closet himself in the cupboard at the bookshop and go over his lines. The conclusion of Steven Parnell's conviction causes a sense of disquiet, as Morse is unyielding in his beliefs. He visits Daley to discuss why Karen Anderson, the supposed last victim of Parnell, had lost her bag six days before Daley finding it at Blenheim.

Daley is next seen driving through the back entrance to Blenheim. The gates would not open for Daley's car without security changes and so consequently, the story changed to Daley following a tractor in. The tractor approaches Blenhiem by a quiet back street in Woodstock. Shortly afterwards, Morse and Lewis are called to Blenhiem to investigate George's death. With the majority of filming taking place in the walled garden, the rest of Blenheim remained open.

The name Blenheim derives from a battle near a small village called Blindheim or Blenheim. John Churchill, the first Duke of Marlborough, won a victory over the forces of Louis XIV, thus saving Europe from French domination.

In reward for his services in defending Holland and Austria from invasion by the French, a grateful Queen Anne granted to Marlborough the Royal Manor of Woodstock and signified that she would build him, at her own expense, a house called Blenheim. Unfortunately, a plan to topple the Malborough's from the Queen's favour succeeded leaving the family to find the finance to complete the building.

Morse and Lewis then go to meet Alan Hardinge at Brasenose. Somehow, they emerge at the gardeners shed in Exeter College.

Morse persists in his belief that Karen Anderson's body is at Wytham Woods and contacts the land registry, but it is at the Foresters Cottage, in woods near Gatwick Airport, that Morse comes face to face with the now Mrs. Michaels. Wytham Woods is in Oxford and although not filmed at, the information relating to the woods as a conservation area is accurate. Apart from the Woods, most of the land is farmland. Raymond Ffennell sold the Estate to the University of Oxford in 1943 and gave the woodlands to the University providing it maintained them as a conservation area.

Karen's hobby had been taking photographs and although the camera was lost, some photographs begin to interest Morse. With determination, he persuades Mrs. Daley to explain the whereabouts of the missing camera. Further photographs see Alan Hardinge, Morse, Lewis, and Dr Muyton at Park Town, Oxford and the story unfolds.

Morse remains resolved that the murder scene is Wytham Woods, due to a corresponding postcard and so the searching begins. On finding a murder victim, but not that of a girl, Leith Hill Woods becomes the focal point for the investigation. Assigning the case alters between Morse and Johnson, Morse is finally left unraveling the missing pieces alone and creating mounting tension between himself and Lewis.

With dinners between Clare and Morse and Morse's awareness of the affair between Clare and Alan, the plot twists and turns reaching a conclusion in the woods.

Morse realizing Lewis is in danger at the forester's cottage and charges through Wytham to Leith Hill, Surrey. It is at the forester's cottage that the dramatic events unfold.

With a sensational culmination of events, Morse indeed does find Karen Anderson, otherwise known as Kate in Leith Woods, otherwise known as Wytham Woods. Here Lewis faces his most challenging time to date.

With a gun pointed firmly in his direction, forced to dig a grave for Karen's husband, Morse saves him. Agonizingly Morse sees the gun kill Karen and as she falls to the floor, Morse is in turmoil.

Also used in Filming

Woodstock, the Blenheim tearooms features in the original Miss Marple.

Harry Potter has been at location at Blenheim Palace recently for a 2007 Production.

THE DAUGHTERS OF CAIN

Aired on the 27th November 1996

Executive Producer Ted Childs

Producer Chris Burt

Directed by Herbert Wise

Writer Julian Mitchell

Production Designer Robin Tarsnane

Location Manager Dennis Firminger

Writer – Novel Colin Dexter

30.

The Oxford skyline slowly descends towards Headington and the John Radcliffe, only to land gently on St. Peter's Hospital, Chertsey, Surrey, as Mrs. Stevens engages Brenda in a lecture on the terminal detriments of smoking outside the hospital. Longsdale College is Wadham College, where eagerly applauded toasts to the Oxford Universities greatness surge through the dinning hall. Julian Mitchell, the writer, has attended Wadham College previously.

Nicholas and Dorothy Wadham, wealthy Somerset landowners, founded Wadham College during the reign of King James I. Although it is one of the youngest of the historic colleges, Wadham has some of the oldest and best-preserved buildings, a result of the rash of rebuilding that occurred throughout Oxford during the 17th century. Wadham also has a claim to fame in that the college's chapel was the first religious building in England to regain its stained glass and statuary following the reformation. Notably, the original statutes forbade women from entering the college, with the exception of a laundress who was to be of 'such age, condition, and reputation as to be above suspicion.' These rules were relaxed over the years, and in 1974, they allowed admission of women as full members of college at all levels. An exasperated Morse sips Glenfiddich as his former college phones in the anticipation of a bequest. The setting adjusts to Ted Brooke's house, found not in Oxford, but in Carpenters Park, North London. Ted Brooke's is annoyed at his wife Brenda's late appearance and violently objects, physically attacking her. Mrs. Stevens is at work at Marston Ferry School, Oxford, quite a way to travel daily from her home near the Brooke's in Carpenter's Park, however reintroducing identifiable Oxford skyline suggests the belief all live close to the discovery of Felix Mc Clure's body. In fact, Felix's body is in Oxford, close to St Giles.

(Photographs courtesy of the owners of Pearce's Coaches)

Following a heart attack, Ted Brooke's admission to Harefield Hospital, Hertfordshire, resumes the link with domestic violence at Brenda's visit. A fact she can barely keep to herself as Mrs. Stevens meets her in the car park.

It is the death of Felix Mc Clure and the promotion of Lewis that presently preoccupies Morse. With stunning architectural views, the scenes change to Tom Quad, Christchurch College, Oxford where Morse talks to Dr. Brownlee about Felix.

Morse learns that the increasingly aggressive ex boxer, Ted Brookes tended to Felix Mc Clure and that a Mathew Rodway had passed away the preceding year by leaping out of a window.

Later Morse discovers he was taking drugs, a piece of information Morse discloses to Lewis as he drives up St Giles to collect him as they join the curator at the Pitt Rivers Museum.

Founded in 1884, when Lt.-General Pitt Rivers, an influential figure in the development of archaeology and evolutionary anthropology, gave his collection to the University, The Pitt Rivers Museum, Oxford hosts an extensive display from the history of tattoos to dinosaurs. So impressive is the extensive exhibitions of historical relics, that they inspired Shelia Hancock and children to visit the museum on the second day and the exact scene from Morse depicting him looking at the shrunken heads later became a prototype for Harry Potter, as ethereal banshees quiver and flicker past a quizzical bus driver. A school party who had booked a visit for the day became extras, an added treat to the curriculum.

During the two days of filming, thirty to forty members of the crew descended on the museum. With little or no natural lighting, the colossal allocated organization of lighting equipment and technology provided the desired appearance, but created a considerable upheaval with intersecting generators and wires. The atmosphere remained congenial and relaxed and the food remarkable. The original scenes show a walk through the Oxford Natural History Museum that leads to the Pitts River where Morse enters into a dialogue regarding their unsavory, temperamental and absent employee caretaker. Morse speaks to the female curator; the basis for the illusory female administrator's character is loosely reliant on the former Administrator of the museum, who retired a few years ago.

In a later visit by Kevin, the surveillance camera was a prop added to the scene. Perhaps explaining why following the alleged theft, the data from the camera remained unchecked. The cabinet does exist, although the works department created a replica for the top that Kevin willfully demolishes. The knife is also authentic when observed in the in the museum with the works department also creating a faithful replica for the later scenes by the river.

The revolutionary system of shadowless movements vital for the script is purely imaginary, as would the idea of a caretaker having access to the keys.

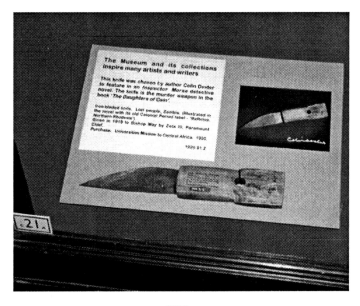

286

Morse and Lewis discuss promotion for Lewis at The Crown, Bray, whilst Ted Brookes willfully flings his dinner across the hospital room and promptly self- discharges. Finding him at home, Morse and Lewis question the Brookes further. Lewis in search of homemade cake the lavish kitchen and equipment impresses Lewis as he fleetingly noticing a photo of Kay Brooks. A similar photo of Kay leads Morse to deliberate with Brownlee. They proceed from the Gates to Christchurch College in Oriel Square, walking into the college with views of the college library in the rear.

As a murder plan hatches at the Brookes house, a transitory hint of Kay purchasing adhesive tape at a local shop in Carpenters Park, London, becomes pertinent later. For the time being, however, she is busy admonishing Ashley at a poolside party. Ashley's father reputedly lived at Blewbury, the setting for the boisterous poolside scenes, in reality it was at Bolney Court, Lower Shiplake near Henley.

The belief in Kevin's expertise prowess and legendary skills of breaking and entering are not lost on Mrs. Stevens, who entices a private exhibition from the hormonal teenager. Later she persuades him to demonstrate his skills at the Pitt Rivers Museum, with half payment now and half afterwards.

The dawning of a sultry summer's day sees Lewis rising early and tirelessly trekking in the shadow of Ashley Davies. He catches up with him across the undulating vastness of the gallops at Seven Barrows Stables, Lambourne, Berkshire.

An example of a Bronze Age cemetery, Seven Barrows lies to the North of Lambourne on the road towards the Ridgeway and Kingston Lisle. Although known as Seven Barrows, the site actually contains twenty- six barrows of various types, dating from about 3800 BC. The barrows themselves are mounds, generally overgrown with grass.

Lewis and Ashley wander along the peacefully snaking road in the direction of the fictitious father's stables, realistically stables owned by Nicky Henderson at the aforementioned Seven Barrows.

In exchanging scenes, Ted Brookes bicycle resurfaces by the Radcliffe Camera, complete with bloodstains whilst Brenda Brookes outwardly blissfully ignorant of any impending tragedy, prepares for a Shakespearean adventure in Stratford on Avon.

As the pace quickens, an optimistic Morse unites with Kay Brookes at Oxford Station, further delighting in consulting with the intellectual, multilingual call girl at the Victoria Arms, Marston, Oxford. As they glide across the Cherwell in a beautifully leisurely punt, harrowing childhood memories reveal a hidden intensity of Brenda's solitary child.

Eagerly accompanied by the weakening Mrs. Stevens, Brenda boards the bus at Marston Ferry School, Oxford. Pearce's coaches supplied the coach for this scene and originally the filming shows outside streetlights, later these cease to exist. As the proprietors of the coach company explain, external shots change and are partially represented by inside studio filming.

(Photograph courtesy of Pearce's Coaches)

Kevin is not on the school trip. Just as the Pitt Rivers Museum is closing, he pays a visit and falsifies a pilfering acquisition of an ancient ceremonial knife, beneath the surveillance of a watchful camera.

As Kevin leaves the museum and impulsively displays his skills of breaking and entering at Carpenters Park, North London. With cheerful abandonment, he ecstatically maneuvers a stolen car recklessly throughout the housing estate, before upturning the vehicle and crashing to a halt.

The hushed sound of Julia echoes compellingly from is lips.

The production designers department, with a lesser contribution at this point from the stunt director, primarily organizes a crash scene. In The Daughters of Cain, Robin Tarsnane was able to choose a location. The directive is that it works for the script, is controllable from a Police point of view, and is safe (from a stunt driver's perspective). With the location manager, the production manager then promotes the idea to the director; finally walking the course with the stunt director who is in charge of the stunt itself. The production manager's vehicle supplier then matches and prepares the stunt car to the car that the character actor drives, in this case a Mark 2 Ford fiesta. Then the petrol tank is detached and substituted with a much smaller strengthened tank and everything likely to fly off if the car rolls. If the end terminates in water then the stripping of everything that is carcinogenic and pollutes is critical i.e. brake lines, fluid bearing pipes/ hydraulics, the engine block etc. On the actual stunt day, police would be controlling traffic, paramedics would be standing by with an ambulance, and if needed, a fire engine. The stunt man alone gets the credit, but behind him is a very dedicated, responsible, and effectual Art Department team that forms the entire breathtaking illusion. As Kevin almost inaudibly utters failing sentimental passion for Julia and the loitering car precariously entombs him, Julia collapses at the school.

Julia recovers sufficiently, however, to hasten to the hospital and defend the honorable moral fiber of the uncommunicative Kevin. Kevin lies in the hospital bed unaware of her visit and seemingly unaware that his incorrectly attached ECG leads could perhaps be an underlying plot to have lethal cardiac drugs administered to Kevin by mistake.

Brenda Brookes is telling Morse of Ted Brookes last movements prior to Ted Brookes missing his hospital appointment, Colin Dexter as Mr. Humphreys is able to fill the gap until Ted Brookes appears at the boathouse near Donnington Bridge, Oxford.

The discovery of the ceremonial knife causes a timely dilemma as murder weapon.

With an additional unlawful death to deliberate, Morse visits Mrs. Stevens. Mrs. Stevens is now in hospital herself and barely capable of any communication, bar gibbering and babbling in melodramatic Shakespearean replies. Her feverish attempts to admit her culpability are fading slowly. Ted had killed Mc Clure and Brenda told Kay, the three women then hatched a plot to seek revenge. An incensed Lewis feels like leaving as Morse explains how although they identified the accessories, no police funds would justify them pursuing an idyllic notion of charging them all. The courts would simply have a preference to the revelation of the killer's identity and no costly trial.

As Morse and Lewis attend Mrs. Steven's funeral, Morse rests his hand on Lewis's shoulder. With a contemptuous glare, Lewis shrugs the affectionate hand from his body and strides into the church. The final scene shows superb acting as a furtive glance at each other restores harmony and the doors slide across the coffin as it disappears from view

Also used in Filming

Lambourne and surrounding areas appeared in Trainer (1991).

DEATH IS NOW MY NEIGHBOUR

Aired on the 19th November 1997

Executive Producer Ted Childs

Producer Chris Burt

Directed by Charles Beeson

Writer Julian Mitchell

Production Designer Robin Tarsnane

Location Manager Alan Pinniger

Writer – Novel Colin Dexter

31.

Cameras pan across the quiet village church, St Nicholas, at Marston. Braziers dairy genuinely supply the milkman on his round. The scene portrays the peace and calm of early morning in Bloxham Drive at Weston Turville, Buckinghamshire. A pony tailed Jeff Owens emerges to greet the day from his home and cheerfully acknowledges the sleepy delights of Rachel as she reaches out to collect the early morning milk delivery from her doorstep. Opposite, Adele Cecil smiles cheerfully as Geoff drives off.

As her neighbour empties the morning's ashes to the bin on a chimneyless estate, an unperturbed Rachel devours her breakfast and prepares for the days work ahead. Her neighbour's suspicions become aroused as she sees a hooded person slink down the alleyway. Unaware of any impending danger, Rachel lazily scoops her hair up into a ponytail, as BBC Radio Oxford plays in the background. The unexpected sound of gunfire reverberates through her blind covered window and her languid thoughts. Maimed, she falls to the floor.

The local residents describe the events surrounding the filming, which was in Brookside, Weston Turville, Buckinghamshire. Four weeks before filming the location manager arrived at one resident's house – complete with I.D. He requested to speak to the husband, who was unavailable at that time and so he returned. On this visit, the wife was out. The couple spoke together later and were totally convinced they were about to appear on a Jeremy Beadle production – not Inspector Morse! The production company wrote to everyone in the immediate area asking if there was any objection to the film company being there for about two weeks. The location vans remained parked in the close for the two weeks with twenty – four hour security, leaving the residents feeling very safe from burglars at the time. Some people rented out their toilets as many of the vans were a fair distance in a local field. They made quite a bit of money from this! With a new road sign erected, they moved to behind the houses where there is a small footpath. The team revamped this with branches, and pieces of tree, made it look quite different. One of the houses had the living room window removed and one with a bullet hole in it appeared. The house were Morse discussed events with the lady putting ashes in the bin, the second garage was used for storing and then completely obliterated by a row of conifer trees added in front of it. The extra's were in their back garden waiting to appear and John Thaw and Kevin Whately later sat on their garden chairs reading their lines and enjoying the bright sunshine. Both John and Kevin were happy to chat to the house owners and sign autographs. The team later removed the window when they left. None of the locals appeared as extras, but there was quite a crowd of local people watching the filming. Children on bicycles and people with dogs suddenly appeared, none of them local.

There were camera tracks laid for the cameras and the production team would stop filming every now and again to allow people to drive their cars in and out. (It was a cul-de-sac). The main scene, took place at night and the neighbour's all gathered in the house opposite to watch the filming. The house used for the character Adele needed redecorating and the team left the decorations in place on leaving. At one point, the jaguar refused to start. John Thaw and Kevin Whately did not arrive until a few minutes before filming started. A transporter brought in the jaguar, later driven a few hundred yards with the rear view mirror removed to allow the cameras to film the actors without obstruction. Morse and Lewis drive the car up to the houses. This shot had to be taken several times. Each time John Thaw and Kevin Whately drove the car up. They then got out of the car, a man employed to drive the car would reverse back the forty or fifty yards. John Thaw and Kevin Whately would walk back to the car and drive back the forty or fifty yards. The pressmen on film were the actual crew. Filming had to stop for a while when a local aircraft from R.A.F Holton flew over.

Mark McGann plays the character of Geoffrey Owens. The house, striped of all furniture and props added for the effect – mainly the office and sitting room. Geoff also appears in the office of the same house, but it gives the outside appearance that he is in Rachel's house when looking out the window. Used in filming, a utility room never actually appeared. For the shooting of Rachel, the filming was in the studio. As described, the window of the house used had the window removed totally and the window with the bullet hole used to replace it. Everyone was very friendly during filming, a community spirit is again the term used, and the food was wonderful. With Mark McGann stopping the prop car to pose for photographs, John Thaw and Kevin Whately would also stop to sign photographs and unbeknown to the cast and crew some of the neighbour's made use of a hole in the fence to take photographs of the filming. With the filming taking four days, the residents would often pop home for lunch to watch filming and then congregate at friends houses during the evening to watch the remainder over a few G & T's.

The local village pub later accommodating and refreshing many of the cast and crew, once filming was over. The outside of a house in Brookside used for Adele, was across the road, but the inside shots were all studio. The footpath to the side of the houses became a rest room for the waiting actors. The extras would wait by the specially constructed Bloxham drive sign. One couple took a photograph of their daughter and husband dancing in their back garden, with the dummy used in filming!

Mill Lane – with field behind for vehicles & equipment.

Field

Footpath

No 22

No 9

(Courtesy of Local Residents)

Alan Pinninger, the location manager for this episode, found this ideal spot for the storyline in Weston Turville. The important factor was a close with an alleyway behind to allow for mistaken identity over a builder's dislike of the number thirteen. The alleyway actually only passes behind two houses before going into fields, but the use of the nearby entrance by a footpath allowed the impression it ran behind the entire street.

The removal of the original fences allowed the creation of holes in the fencing, with new fences erected following the filming. With the location manger's love of houses on a corner to give depth of field apparent, it also supplied the requirement for modern houses to embrace the characters lifestyles.

Following a short repartee with his superior, Morse discusses developments concerning senior changes relating to the new April budget and the realistic prospects of promotion for Lewis. Despondent at the prospect for Lewis' future in the police force, Morse joins the expanding crime scene at Bloxham Drive to discover a valentine card.

The setting changes to the bedroom of Dennis and Shelly Cornfield. A passionate embrace signifies the profound devotion between the Oxford Don and his newfound American wife. The now spent ardor causes the tardy arrival of Dennis at a meeting to decide on the contestants for the thirty- fifth Don of Lonsdale. As the characters enter Brasenose College by the eye-catching Radcliffe Camera, they immediately materialize in Oriel College.

The opposing contestant rings his intoxicated wife, who celebrates her determination for his impending promotion with a further tipple or two. Cornfield, however, seeks the company and rumours of Dora, as they cross the Oriel College Quad.

Adele admires the talents of her pupil vocalist at Magdalen College School, Oxford. With the focused dedication of a coach, she is intense on the melodious task and so oblivious to Morse entering the room. Morse and Adele leave the novice soloist to saunter in affectionate camaraderie through the scenic gardens of Magdalen School, Oxford. Unhurriedly Morse and Adele stroll through the lush foliage. Slowly bonding, they gently deliberate on the day's events. Adele sketchily discloses Rachel and Julian's affair, declining to mention a former relationship between her and Dennis.

Jeff Owens, meanwhile, is actively engaged in coordinating interviews of the opposing Dons. Within the offices of The Oxford Mail, Osney Mead, Oxford, he zealously sets dates and times before meeting his girlfriend for lunch at Le Petit Blanc, Jericho, Oxford. It is at Osney Mead, that Morse later discovers the expensive flamboyant lifestyle of the roguish, amorous Jeff is beyond his salary. The discovery leads to the exposure of blackmail and deceit, providing a potent motive for murder.

Entering by the side door Morse and Lewis enjoy a liquid lunch at The Crown, Bray. Later in the episode, they revisit The Crown entering by the front door, giving the facade of two different establishments.

Julian seems somewhat distasteful at the discovery of his step - daughter and wife together at his home at East Molsey, Surrey. Hushed voices subside as he nears. Forceful comments over favours asked deviously disperse. Indeed, Julian emulates a certain Machiavellian feeling to explanations over appointments with his physiotherapist in later discussions with Morse. Afterwards, an amused Angela verifies Julian explanation of an alibi for the time of Rachel's murder and a planned trip to Bath.

Shelley is intent on building a home for herself and Dennis and Clixby accompanies her in her quest. It is Clixby's intentions that incense Shelley, although later driven by superseding ambition she was more agreeable to his sexual demands.

Lewis and Morse convene to discuss their thoughts on the case. Morse adamant that the murderer is a man and rejects any implication Lewis arouses over Adele. Unaware of the discussion Adele arrives home to see Dennis visit Jeff, before Dennis runs past a canal to his own home in Bramley, Near Guilford, Surrey.

Serving breakfasts in Bath, the importance of one laden with sweet delights and one devoid of all sweet contents seems unimportant.

Languishing splattered in blood; Jeff seems to have missed breakfast and his meeting at the races. The bittersweet delights of revenge are outlined a detached mother's face. Frustration now etches the contours of Morse's face as he journeys through the centre of Oxford weekend drivers and tourists the cause of his irritation. Further infuriated by the police officer's lack of effort in perceiving the proximity of murder, he ponders the pathologists quip over the number thirteen. With duplicated ponytails and the builders dislike of thirteen it seems to provide an answer. Certainly it provides the initials AM –DC–CB which suggest a clue to the funding behind Jeff's prosperous existence. Shelley, though, is busy purchasing a dress from Hobbs, Little Clarendon Street, Oxford.

Newspaper cuttings attract the attention of Morse, with Kevin Martin flight from his wife and daughter aboard an ocean bound vessel. Amongst his baggage, the discovery by his wife and daughter of a replacement in his affections lead to his ultimate death. Angela Martin, his wife, later becoming Angela Storrs.

Lewis has urgent family business to attend to and Shelley reluctantly entertains Clixby. Shelly belatedly realizing this will not advance her husbands career, but simply provide retribution for Clixby after Dennis's affair with his wife.

Lewis that feels the need for a coffee as Angela is also is in need of revival in time for the gathering at Brasenose College. Colin Dexter appears with a speaking part at the college. Dennis, however, learning of his wife's betrayal is broken hearted. He pursues her until an untimely fall leaves Shelley fatally exhausted.

Morse does pay attention to Lewis's concerns about Adele, but on questioning she offers an incentive to make it up to her for getting it wrong. Adele wishes to know Morse's first name. Morse has never revealed this to anyone before and responds

"My whole life's effort resolves around Eve, 9 letters"

With a visit to The Royal Crescent Hotel in Bath, Morse uncovers the supplementary breakfasts. Examining single woman occupancy, Morse discovers the link between Angela Storrs and Dianna Cunningham. As Morse completes his crossword, he refers to A-Z crosswords being the best in the world – Colin Dexter sets crosswords under the name A-Z. Along with the crossword, Morse uncovers both the motive and the murderer. He returns to Oxford giving Clixby little alternative to resigning. Arriving at The Crown, Bray, Morse listens to Adele's cryptic response. With parental beliefs as Quakers and a fatherly esteem for Captain Cook, Inspector Morse is Inspector Endeavour Morse. Lewis's expression says it all before Morse and Adele return to the Royal Bath Hotel, Bath. Here they walk arm in with an affectionate smile as they enter the hotel.

THE WENCH IS DEAD

Aired on the 11th November 1998

Executive Producer Ted Childs

Producer Chris Burt

Directed by Robert Knights

Writer Malcolm Bradbury

Production Designer Robin Tarsnane

Location Manager Alan Pinniger

Writer – Novel Colin Dexter

32.

An agitated Morse mops his damp forehead, beads of sweat forming as he joins Colin Dexter and Robert Gasser at the historical Oxford Crime Exhibition at Wadham College, Oxford. Quietly debating Dr Van Buren's lecture of the events surrounding the Oxford Canal Murders he uncharacteristically refuses a drink and scurries to the bathroom. Violent scarlet streams of blood trickle down the clean white basin as Morse sinks to the ground. Rushed by ambulance to St Peter's Hospital, Chertsey, Morse resides reluctantly in the pristine bed. Seemingly a gown from the John Radcliffe has found its way to Chertsey at the same time as Morse!

Dr Van Buren later visits him with a copy of her book The Oxford Canal Murders, which takes precedence over the more mundane book supplied by Kershaw. Suitably inspired, Morse delves into the policing techniques of the1859 force and finds unanswered questions, which naturally he feels obliged to investigate. As he reads the literature behind the murders, the episode changes to encompass the feel of bygone days, with barge scenes from the canal taken from Daventry to Oxford. The story unfolds of the events leading to the hanging of the Boatmen in the Oxford Canal Murders. As Inspector Morse lies grief stricken in his hospital bed, the ulcer has ceased to worry him but the century's old plight of the boatmen hanged for the murder of Joanna Franks is. As he drifts into nostalgia, Adele arrives at the new modernized Oxford Railway Station.

Having established a motive as an insurance claim and the murder spectacularly performed by illusion, Morse gains the co-operation not of Lewis, but of Kershaw- a fast track police graduate lent to him, relieving Strange of a zealous tea boy. From hospital bed to canal side, he sets out to prove that the boatmen of the Barbara Bray, hanged for what became the 1859 Oxford Canal Murders, were innocent characters in The Great Donovan Insurance Extravaganza. Notably, whilst in hospital a few vanishing and re appearing tricks seem to occur – namely the posters on the wall behind the nurse's station!

The episode flips between present time and the telling of the Oxford Canal Murders. The story originates from a real murder on the Trent and Mersey canal. The murder Of Christina Collins took place at the canal in 1839 at a place known locally as the 'bloody steps' the canal at Brindley Bank near Rugeley, Staffordshire. As they pulled her body from the water, blood ran down a flight of steps leading from the canal. Today the stain occasionally reappears and the Christina still reputedly haunts the site.

The renaming of the original barge Australia, involved adding bolt on boards on one side. A professional barge painter employed for the artistic effects, the results transformed the era. At the Randolph Hotel Adele persuades Strange to humour Morse in his search and Kershaw joins Morse in his quest for the truth. Kershaw's visits to the department of Criminology, Wellington Square, Off St John's Road, Oxford and the Bodlean continue to uncover facts that perturb Morse in his pursuit. Robert Gasser has a speaking part as the librarian. With the team considering his voice too loud for a librarian and is dubbed over. Kershaw and Dr Van Buren do discuss the case at length walking through The Grove, of Trinity College, Oxford.

Amid many references to Morse's retirement and indications of his failing health, Morse occupies his intellectual requirements with the story of the Oxford Canal Murders.

Joanna Franks boarded the Barbara Bray at the Black Country Museum. Called Toohley's Boatyard, Banbury in the script, the boatyard does exist – now preserved in the midst of a large shopping complex.

The public face of the Museum is the open-air visitor attraction set in the heart of the industrial West Midlands. Visitors are free to wander around the 'Living Museum', an urban heritage park, where buildings and structures have been rebuilt to tell the story of this part of The Black Country, as the heartland of industrial Britain. The core of the Museum is the village area built around the canal that runs into Dudley Tunnel and the adjacent canal basin. The village is entered over a cast and wrought iron bridge which originally stood in Wolverhampton, and on either side of the main street are shops and houses, including the Chemist's, General Store, Pawnbrokers', a 1930's Fried Fish Shop and The Bottle and Glass Public House which was moved from Buckpool in Brierley Hill. Along the cobbled Coppice Street stand workers' cottages from the late 18th Century and the back-to-back houses of 1850.

Her husband had journeyed to London for employment as an Osteller. She was to join him in the least expensive way – aboard the Barbara Bray. Already concerning Morse, he knew from Kershaw that there is little difference in the cost of various modes of transport and the barge was the slowest of these means. A short interlude, again at the Black Country Museum sees Joanna complaining to the proprietor about the lewd ways of the boatman, although she seems content to rejoin them on their journey.

(Pictures courtesy of The Black Country Living Museum)

As the journey continues with the drunken merriment atop of the barge, in the background the distinctive shapes of the hills from Pewsey along to Wooton Rivers are on the other side of Bruce's Tunnel, Wiltshire.

With the next scenes calling for a lonely angler investigating the sounds of a large splash and discovering the body of a woman in the muddy waters, the location area changes to the side of the Barge Inn, Honey Street, Pewsey, Wiltshire. Originally, there was a small pier, which still is visible in the filming. Today, Wiltshire is famous for its crop circles and the Barge Inn in today's times enjoys a clientele of 'croppies'. Just behind the pub was a field of tents, each tent seemingly fully equipped with satellite tracking equipment-projecting skywards through the canvas, an intriguing sight!

The Barge Inn has remained unchanged for centuries in addition, was originally an alehouse, with a mill, grocery, bakery, slaughterhouse, and wharf, meeting all of the boatmen's needs. On searching the whole length of the Kennet & Avon, the Barge offered an authentic and unchanged since 1810 abattoir to the side of the pub.

With a little algae paint added, it was ideal for the storyline. Fortunately, the pub also had a campsite to the back, which provided the much-needed space for parking and caravans.

A website for The Barge Inn shows pictures taken during the filming of Inspector Morse.

(Photographs courtesy of Adrian and June Potts, The Barge Inn)

Transformation of the Inn for the scenes recalling the actual murder included adding straw, peat and hay to cover the ground. A shed built to the front of the building cost £2,000 and plastic wisteria added to the front of the pub transformed the building. Blackened windows showed no curtaining or reflections. Even six chickens arrived to complete the image, although heard, they were very difficult to see!

The landlord kindly had bought new outdoor seating for the modern scenes, but the crew never used them and they remained piled behind a hedge until after filming.

The detailed transformation of the abattoir includes rabbits hanging from the original hooks. As the door opens, it cleverly misses the Vale of Pewsey White Horse etched in the hills - an inch more would reveal all. It took five days of filming, however all areas were left exactly as found. New plants at the front of the pub replacing ones damaged ones during the transformation.

The jaguar played a small cameo role and it was brought in and placed in front of the pub for one scene - although never driven it was however continuously polished ready for it's appearance.

Recollections from the crowd gathered at the barn tell of a sinister figure of a tall man walking away along the canal as they hear the sound of something falling into the water. The requirements where for a quiet area in order to set the scene and the canal from Bruce's Tunnel towards Great Bedwyn offered solitude and were devoid of any noise apart from the nearby railway line and a train approximately every twenty minutes, which could be worked around. Richard Hill on location for the day reports how the peace of an unperturbed barge continuing into the mist is disturbed as a transformation of the landscape occurs. Already muddy paths acquire an array of black bags filled with liquid nitrogen and covered by leaves for the actors to walk on. The surrounding area covered by mist, modern signs covered with foliage and although filmed during the day -it appeared to be night. The natural twists and turns hiding from view any unwanted superfluous shots, it provided the location for many of the original views. Although the story unfolds on the Oxford Canal, the barges were too big to go alongside and so team used the Kennet & Avon. Called The Prince's Cut in the film it suggests the location is Duke's Cut, just outside Oxford, but in reality, it is Bedwyn.

Further, afield the production team was preparing yet another area, Braunston No 2 lock, Northamptonshire. It is here – called Filbert lock in the episode – that Joanna escapes to meet with her husband in the woods nearby. Cloaked in darkness, the corpse of another woman waits to take Joanna place. Tim Coghlan describes the events of the day.

As Joanna disappears into the murky waters and resurfaces to begin life anew with her husband, the police are catching up with the boatmen at Brauston marina. The scenes of Joanna in the water were at The Barge Inn. A stuntwoman was paid £100 each time she entered the water. Financially rewarding, as the shot took eleven takes. At Brauston Marina, Tim Coghlan describes how the Victorian era was replicated with the aid of many a prop. As transportation from a long gone era arrives, the team had set to work on the lock keepers cottage adding black tape to reduce the window sizes with taped crosses. Elemental straw, sand, dust and grime is scattered to put the last touches on the 140-year-old transformation.

Meanwhile the barges from the previous days filming at the Black Country Museum travel down to join the cast and crew. With the initial work done, actors in all guises arrive, fresh for the start of the days filming of the entrapment of the boatmen from the Barbara Bray.

As the action begins, one of the two horses hired for the day, Dominic, became very mistrustful of the camera operators and crew entailing the owner concealing their presence behind him whilst filming.

The barge, with no engine to stop it, was difficult to manoeuvre, often dragged into position, narrowly missing the canal sides. Hurriedly gathered advice meant the police officers tying the boat to a bollard However, the days events had taken there toll and weary actors played out their roles. One actor raising temperatures as he fought to deliver his speech several times, before the light finally faded.

In the storyline, the boatmen go from the barge at Brauston to the courtroom in Oxford and many twists then decide their fate. The court scenes are actually at the old courtroom, St Albans Town Hall.

With various flashbacks throughout the episode, the dark paneled walls surround the deliberating judge. Closeted into the packed courtroom, the stench of fear rises as the interrogation of the boatmen unfolds.

This includes reminiscing over the events that led up to the fatal day, from Joanna embarking on her fateful journey to her loud debauchery onboard and audible complaints at the crucial moments. As a distressed bereaved husband identifies her dead body, how could anyone disbelieve or have any skepticism towards the sincerity in their voices- both past and present - against those of a drunken, callous, lecherous, heathen bunch?

The fervor and claustrophobic atmosphere reaches a pinnacle, pronounced guilty, the boatmen somberly adjourn to the gallows at Oxford Jail. Now redeveloped as part of the Malmaison Hotel Group, Oxford Jail remains, with many of the original features are still evident.

Despite an austere Scottish nurse leaving Morse high and dry without intravenous infusion whilst nil by mouth overnight, he survives the hospital visit. Finally arriving home, a recuperating, but skeptical Morse decides to discuss the book at length with Dr Van Buren. With a little flirtatious help Kershaw locates Joanna's trunk and Morse and Adele discover the false bottom. It takes a woman's intuition to question the lack of contents and the carpetbag. With medical records of the time, Morse and Kershaw discuss the case with Dr. Laura Hobson. Cut Victorian knickers, small shoes and the hem being let down on the gown suggest the dress were for a larger woman of a lesser height. Dr Van Buren watches as Morse tries to exhume the body of Joanna Franks in St. Sepulcre's Cemetery Jericho, Oxford.

Morse is convinced that the insurance money collected at the time of her death had made her move elsewhere, not the newly erected flats! Kershaw joins Morse and Dr Van Buren at The Crown Inn, Bray as Morse painstakingly recounts all the facts as he sees them. Dr. Van Buren leaves from Oxford Railway Station, seen by Adele.

Adele and Morse discuss the crossword as realization over anagrams dawn. The scenes change to The Lyceum, London for the magical mystery that was Great Donovan. Yet, it takes a journey to Bertnaghboy Bay, Ireland and a bagful of tricks to finally exhume the illusion and resurrect substantiation of Morse's unlikely theory as truth and justice win through.

As the turbulent Irish Sea, laps furiously against the shoreline as Morse and Adele set out to unfold the mystery that surrounds the great Irish extravaganza.

Following the winding coastal roads around the small peninsula to calmer waters, they climb the brow of a hill. Anticipation mounting, the scenery unfolds and the breath taking beauty of the white washed village nestling in the hillside unfolds.

317

Lying beyond the white buildings is the church and graveyard. As Morse and Adele make their way to the quaint church, silhouetted against the coastline they reach the tiny village where Morse visits the local police with an exhumation request. The cost of a few bottles of whiskey secures the help of the local Irish lads in their thirsty grave digging.

The sea glistens as a grave area begins to yield its buried secrets. With the whistling sound of the waves in the background, a gentle wind tickles at Morse's silver hair. Waiting for the evidence to be unearthed, Morse and Adele share an enchanted stroll along the eye -catching coastline. Hand in hand in a magical moment of tenderness and affection, they await the verdict on the death of the great impressionist.

The twists and tails of many centuries surrender their stony silence, yet the perhaps enigma of the legendary Irish charm has a mystery of its own to divulge?

With illusion the theme of the episode, the team adds a little chimera themselves. The charming Irish coastline and villages are not in fact Ireland at all, but the idyllic parish of Aberdaron, North Wales. The church is St Hywyn's Church.

Robin Tarsane, the production designer on this episode, found the episode most interesting as designing a period drama is always more challenging than a contemporary one. The team never felt they would find such a location overlooking the sea in Ireland. With a few changes though, Aberdaron certainly fitted the bill. They wanted to dig a grave in the churchyard, but were unable to do so as it was full. They were able to dig one just over the wall and make it look like an extension to the graveyard, with their own gravestones dressing the area. With two of the finest actors to work with, Morse was great fun to work on and the professional team worked hard, but had fun.

A short history of the church explains why this particular church was ideal for the scene. Only two churches meet the criteria. One in Ireland and one in Wales, Wales was a more cost effective choice. There has been a place of Christian worship at the edge of the sea at Aberdaron since the fifth century. St Hywyn's was first a simple wooden structure that housed both Hywyn and his prayer cell. From here, preaching of the Gospel reached villagers. These were a few villagers whose humble cottages clung to the side of the cliffs and whose livelihood depended on the sea and the few acres of soil in which they grew crops. Cadfan, the warrior saint, who traveled from Brittany with Hywyn, moved on to Enlli, the island off the tip of the Llŷn peninsula. There he set up a religious house, later to be dedicated to St Mary. To both men these were places of their resurrection. Places where they felt God had called them to live, to pray, and to die. In 1137, Gruffydd ap Cynan, King of Gwynedd, began erecting stone churches to replace the wooden buildings in the most important parishes and so the oldest portion of St Hywyn's Church dates from this time.

As a sanctuary church, it had a stone chair called the chair of peace. This allowed settling disputes and a sanctuary for fugitives for forty days and nights. Enlarged in 1417, the church at Aberdaron continued. The Reformation in 1536 saw the monasteries closed by Henry VIII and for a short while the Diocese of Bangor benefited from a revitalized church served by devout priests, but gradually decline set in and sinecure rectors with no parish duties to perform were in charge and paid vicars to take on the duties of parish priest. In 1624, St John's College, Cambridge became the patron of the parish and remained so for almost 300 years. The church building had fallen into a poor state of repair by the late 18th century. The 19th century saw restoration a further refurbishment in 1906. The churchyard later increased in size. By the late 20th century, the church was again in need of restoration. The new sea defense, to stop the churchyard slipping onto the beach, had been completed, but the building itself is in need of preservation and re-pointing to prevent salt damage continuing.

Only the soft sounds of the waves, the song of the seals and the cries of the sea birds accompany the timelessness of this holy place.

The sixty -strong crew filmed for three days in the area. With the crew staying at the Hotels in Aberdaron, the cast were staying at nearby Abersoch a local taxi firm transported them back and forth. The village car park became saturated with the paraphernalia and vehicles associated with filming. Wires trailed throughout the engulfed village streets. The Ship Inn acquired false Guinness signs on the windows that remain today, alongside a green doorway and Irish signs. A local house became the police station and villagers flocked to see the filming.

Shelia Hancock reputedly joined the team.

John Thaw spent half an hour in each village pub with half a Guinness. He also visited the local shop and spent time answering the local's questions and requests for autographs. The landlord of the Ship Inn had to open the doors at four in the morning ready for the day's filming, not easy for the crew following a late night sampling the delights of the bar! A bacon sandwich from the location catering suppliers helped to rebalance the rude awakening. Many film and T.V stars had visited the area for filming, but John Thaw remained remembered fondly for the time he spent getting to know the area and the people who loved and worked there.

An illusionary gravestone made of polystyrene and cardboard provided the head stone in an area to the front of the small church where the exhumation of the theatrical grave took place.

The mystical moments are certainly powerful as Morse and Adele share a potent magic of their own. Conjuring a romantic feel, the episode gently reaches a conclusion capturing a compassionate charismatic ambiance captivating not only Morse and Adele, but every viewer as well.

Also Used in Filming

St Albans Town Hall Court room also appears in Eastenders and Casualty. August (1996).

During the early part of October 2006, John Nettles and sixty cast and crew spent five days filming at Cwm Dyli, along the valley from Llyn Gwynant, Snowdonia and local farms. Leaning out of a hovering helicopter as part of a riveting final scene in Midsommer Murders, the dramatic action will reach the television screens in 2007.

THE REMORSEFUL DAY

Aired on the 15th November 2000

Executive Producer Ted Childs

Producer Chris Burt

Directed by Jack Gold

Writer Stephen Churchett

Production Designer Robin Tarsnane

Location Manager Alan Pinniger

Writer – Novel Colin Dexter

33.

The opening scenes are not of Oxford, but of a house in Lower Swinstead – the location being St Hubert's, Gerrards Cross, Buckinghamshire. A dark sinister house that provides the backdrop to a story, which winds its way around plots that include disturbing sexual overtones and a murder. The camera pans stylish silverware on a table, resting for a moment on a devoted family photograph, before zooming to a shot of the mother softly singing Unchained Melody. With affection, she reads a letter from Morse. Later this letter is to cause Strange some deliberation.

Concealed in the bushes a man crouches watching the house, by his side implements suggesting an attempted burglary lay idle as he watches a guest arrive. The mother suggestively welcomes the guest into her home. As suggestively, she appears in a dream Morse awakens from suddenly and clutches his chest. A sad farewell letter from Adele leaves Morse at home, alone, bird watching. Morse is soon is relaxing as Lewis arrives laden with classical gifts and information on bird watching.

Sandra answers the telephone at her home and is dispirited at being let down as an elderly man hurriedly takes a taxi home to his ominous Lower Swinstead family home. As he enters, there are no alarms heard.

A gripping turn of attention focuses on Morse in a black trouser suit standing on the driveway with the powerful setting of the gloomy trees and bright moon behind him, outlining his looming materialization. The scenes travel to the bedroom where the bonded mother lays butchered. Morse flashes back to the woman nursing him oblivious of a letter handed to his superior at the scene of the crime. Yvonne Harrison, the woman killed at the family home had been dead a year and someone was writing letters suggesting further clues to her murder was about to unfold.

Harry Rep's imminent departure from prison, with Morse back to work the next day, leaves Lewis hot on the trail from Bullington Prison to Bicester Bus Station and onto Bay 2, Gloucester Green, Bus Station. Oxford.

Unfortunately, Lewis mislays him whilst Tesco's proves too alluring, with freshly printed football results and is none too pleased at Morse's trail.

Morse is with Sandra Harrison, at St. Peter's Hospital, Chertsey, a doctor taking his Blood Pressure, Yvonne's mother. Lewis meanwhile is at Debbie Rep's house in New Denham, Buckinghamshire, only to find he is only following Morse's footsteps. Not too happy he rejoins him as they quench their thirst at the Victoria Arms, Old Marston, Oxfordshire. A technique known as using the magic moment captures the beautiful lighting at this point.

The scenes then travel to Wapsley Wood Landfill Site, Gerrards Cross for the discovery of Paddy Flynn, the taxi driver who supplied an alibi for Mr. Harrison. One surmises that the reality of the smell is truly authentic!

Whilst Debbie unpacks groceries and a welcome home card for her husband at Willowbank Village, New Denham, his late arrival leaves her unperturbed though and she is soon entertaining the local builder. The discovery of a second body at the Boathouse, Oxford (the Trout Inn seen in the background), means work for Morse and Lewis. The alarming sounds at the boathouse begin to register a need to investigate further.

With Morse now officially back at work and in charge of the case, Lewis's crestfallen face shows his disappointment. Meanwhile, as Sandra leaves the hospital, Lionel receives a well-aimed slap before she joins her family for lunch at the Randolph Hotel. The imagination leads to white napkins discreetly replaced at each move, and a delicate mouthwatering explosion of tantalizing tastes soothing the palate as the feast unfolds conveying beautiful works of art delicately placed on the pristine plates. A meal at the Randolph is an unforgettable experience.

Morse has to tell Harry rep's widow, Debbie that he is dead. She laughs at the suggestion of sex and Harry, but describes Yvonne as a scrubber in a posh house. Peeved by her description of Yvonne, Morse leaves. Lewis has discovered money at Flynn's bed-sit and the suspicion is now turning to blackmail. A teenager cycles in the car park of the Queens Arms, Little Marlow, Buckinghamshire – almost run over by the builder John Barron.

John Barron then continues to 33, Sheep Street, Burfield and falls from a ladder, knocked by a man in a red tracksuit – later found in a charity shop on The High, Oxford.

It is at Thorton's bookshop, Oxford, now the Buttery that Morse interviews Sandra's brother, Simon Harrison.

The owner describes how 'humble' John Thaw seemed, whilst filming he asked to be allowed to go to a quiet room to go over his lines and ensconced himself in a small back room. Not having any Morse's titles in stock at the time, a desperate dash to the local shops secured some paperback copies, which John Thaw signed. The day was quite chaotic, some book -cases not having the right 'look' for the scenes. The producer complete with carpenter appeared to make new bookcases, which they left after filming. The shop sign notably changed to read Harrison's. Some of the shop owners in Broad Street were unaware of the impending filming and the partial closure of the street to shoppers whilst filming. It left a few angry proprietors over loss of revenue!

Red kites and deaf men telling lies accumulate with an arrest. Yet, Wesley Smith prompts a young teenager to visit the police station and Simon's lip reading skills and admits to what happened. The home of the teenager is found on a council estate at new Denham, the inside one house, the outside another. Morse briefly encounters him. Again, he is in the car park at the Queen's Head, Little Marlow.

Morse also visits a packing Sandra bound for Heathrow Airport. Intriguingly, Morse then sees Dexter at Magdalen College Café Terrace, in a wheelchair, although genuinely there is no wheelchair access, before he is on his way to attend John's funeral at St. Mary the Virgin, Fawley Church, Buckinghamshire. A church often commandeered for filming as the local community contains many people from the acting world.

It is from a cherry picker firmly routed in the then Spice Girl Mel B's garden that the wake scenes at the Queen's Head, Little Marlow are filmed and following the funeral Morse goes to relax at home with a whiskey. With it arranged to leave his body to medical science, Morse is morose as he listens to his classical music, he switches it off and listens to the clock ticking in the silence.

Morse arrives at choir rehearsals at Exeter College. Talking to Lionel brings back painful memories, but nothing as painful as the pain now in Morse's arm, as Lionel mimes to 'Libera Me' by Gabriel Faure. With the aid of a prop bought into Exeter College, he phones Lewis. The harmonious chords of Fare's Requiem, conducted by Barrington Pheloug float melodiously through the air as a distressed Inspector Morse walks across the quad. Mopping a fevered brow, he clutches his chest in anguish as In Paressum plays heartrendingly in the background. The choir was Exeter College choir, a closed set with few people able to watch and the flowers genuine, few props at this stage. The graceful spire of Exeter's Chapel Tower stretches skywards, birds flap nosily disturbed by the events and as people run in slow motion towards him, Inspector Morse abruptly collapses to the ground.

As sirens wail despondently, the ambulance appears from the Tower area of Exeter College, it travels through what is affectionally now known as the dustbin quad and to a collapsed Morse on the quad outside the chapel. The ambulance had been waiting outside the unlocked gates and on cue; the head porter at that time imitates opening the gates to allow the ambulance entrance. The filming for the events took place from the top of the buildings opposite.

One story reads that a quirk of filming, never happened before, resulted in a jammed camera, meaning this shot had to be taken five times. However, an extra at the time does not recall the event – perhaps this is another Morse mystery? Speaking to Chris Burt, he describes that the spooky event did indeed take place.

Lewis and Strange accompany Morse to the hospital and as Morse waits for the lift, he sees a man on crutches, providing him with the answers.

As Morse with dying breath whispers "Thank Lewis for me", Lewis is solving the case at Heathrow Airport; tearfully he retorts to Sandra that Morse is dead.

Promptly transferred to A & E at St. Peter's Hospital, Chertsey, Surrey, featured as the Radcliffe in Oxford. Inspector Morse's heart attack was in Oxford, outside Exeter College chapel, but contrary to popular belief, Inspector Morse died at St Peter's Hospital, Chertsey, Surrey.

With cast and crew alike in tears, Lewis visits the morgue where Inspector Morse's body lies on the morgue table. Both Morse and Lewis form a solitary forlorn image.

It is with tearful endurance that Lewis can barely withdraw the sheet back and reluctantly, hesitatingly and with great sorrow, Lewis bends over to kiss Morse, quietly murmuring "Goodbye Sir" – a poignant, tear evoking moment for all. Silence descends as the misty, dreamy spires of Oxford provide the backdrop as a melancholy Lewis leaves, no longer with Morse beside him.

AN INSPECTOR CALLS AT ST.PETER'S.

(KINDLY REPRODUCED WITH PERMISSION BY SHELIA FERGUSON, PRESS OFFFICER, ST. PETER'S HOSPITAL, CHERTSEY).

"Some of you will have noticed, others may not...... but for bits of one week in April, we were temporarily transferred from St. Peter's, Chertsey to the John Radcliffe Hospital, Oxford .. all by the magic of television. Carlton television spent 2 days setting up and four full days filming the scenes that follow Inspector Morse's admission into hospital and his final days.

Carlton television used St. Peter's for the filming of some crucial and poignant scenes for the 33rd and final Inspector Morse.

The empty Elliot Ward in the Abbey Wing was the main location for most of the filming – at various times it became a Coronary Care Unit, a Gastroenterology Clinic and even a consultant's office. (although much too spacious to be realistic!).

The Abbey Wing staff found a novel way of beating the NHS cuts- they got their windows cleaned free of charge by the film crew! They spent a couple of days cleaning both the inside and outside of the reception windows to improve their exterior shots. Unfortunately, when they left they did remember to take with them the potted plants and benches that had dressed the outside of the Abbey Wing – but it did look nice while it lasted!

Having a crew of about 80 people bringing with them vast amounts of equipment necessitated a lot of hard work and co-operation between the various departments to ensure things went as smoothly as possible with as little disruption to the day-to- day work of the hospital. The Elliot Ward wasn't the only place to see action; scenes were shot in A & E Resuscitation Area – luckily, the filming took place on an unusually quiet morning – Operating Theatre 1, the mortuary, the main reception area and the League of Friends Shop.

The film crew needed almost as much constant attention as normal patients! At various times they needed keys to locked windows; replacement lightbulbs; the air conditioning turned off; the lights turned on; eight matching counterpanes; 15 matching chairs; cars moved; drilling stopped etc! Our staff coped amazingly well with all the extra unusual requests.

By far the most difficult request to meet was – perhaps not surprisingly 'can we have 10 empty beds'. As you know, this is not an easy task in an NHS hospital these days! When the crew first started their recce visits, Elliot Ward had a full compliment of beds. Unfortunately since then and the filming date most of the beds had disappeared one by one, those left were devoid of their mattresses. However, the portering staff rose to the challenge and by the time the crew started filming, the elusive empty beds were back in place 1. The only easy task was finding rooms for the stars to rest in-between takes… for some reason no one ever refused to give up their office for that!

The crew became very adept at swapping St. Peter's signs for those of the John Radcliffe and then speedily putting them back in their normal places so that no one but the film crew noticed the difference. But, I am sure you will when you watch the programme. The road one-way system was changed; the mortuary door, corridor, and Elliot Ward are almost certainly unrecognizable!

The stars, John Thaw, Kevin Whately, and James Grout were all on site. They were joined by T P McKenna and Anna Wilson- Jones (who had just finished appearing as 'Justine' in Monarch of the Glen). During the exterior scenes outside the Abbey Wing the cast, members posed for photographs and signed autographs for staff and patients. Even the classic red jaguar made an appearance as John Thaw recorded a piece for a National Television Awards Ceremony.

No problem with the patients and visitors – they all seemed fascinated by what was going on. At times, it was a little difficult working out who were the real patients and visitors and who the thirty or more extras were.

I did spend a lot of time apologizing to visitors about the filming only to be told they weren't really visitors and I did overhear one nurse telling one actor in a dressing gown that he really should be back on the ward and not outside in the cold air!.

A delighted film crew remained enthusiastic about how well everything had gone and they clearly appreciated the help they got form staff. The location manager sent a special thank—you letter, in which he said he had filmed in a good many hospitals but had never known such good humour and kindness from the staff. To emphasis this afterwards, beside the standard fee, they sent bouquet of flowers to various areas as well as a generous cheque to the League of Friends.

So when all you Morse fans do sit down to watch 'The Remorseful Day' in the autumn, don't spend all your time trying to work out where it was all filmed... but whatever you do, don't forget your box of tissues. You will need them – some very moving scenes been shot in the hospital.

Finally … as you might expect, amongst all the hard work there was the odd 'funny' moment! One elderly lady reunited with her husband at the time receiving in the A & E Resuscitation could not resist greeting the poor patient not with 'how are you dear', but instead with a very excited 'did you know John Thaw is in the bed next to you?'

Shelia Ferguson. *ASPire Ashford & St Peter's Information Review.* Morse Gets Dashed at St. Peter's. Summer Issue 2000.

Also Used in Filming

St Hubert's lends itself perfectly to some of the following locations. The Persuaders (1970), The New Avengers (1976), The Professionals (1979/80/81), Hammer House of Mystery and Suspense (1983), Island of Terror (1966), The League of Gentlemen (1960) and the video of the group The Pretenders 'Don't Get Me Wrong'.

THE CIRCUS COMES TO TOWN

Aired on the 29th January 2006

Executive Producer Ted Childs

Producer Chris Burt

Directed by Bill Anderson

Writer Stephen Churchett, Russell Lewis

Production Designer Robin Tarsnane

Location Manager Alan Pinniger

Based on the characters in the novels of Colin Dexter

34

It is with great sadness that the world learnt that John Thaw died in February 2002. An exceptional actor that brought unique energy and soul to every character he portrayed. Nobody could ever replace him, nor would anyone try.

With the public blessing of Shelia Hancock, the characters of Colin Dexter and the talented production team, an understandably nervousness Kevin Whately began filming the new episode of Lewis.

Appealing references firmly put this as not usurping the role of Inspector Morse, but as time moving on. With poignant, sentimental reminders jolting the new Inspector into the progressive Oxford Police Force (not the Thames Valley), as the circus, again, comes to town.

With everything checked and doubled checked in the time honoured tradition, filming started on Monday 18 July 2005.

The time-honored, comfortable opening scenes span the Oxford skyline in the long-established scene-setting mode. Deafening music reels throughout the quad at Wadham College as Danny Griffon is introduced frantically scribbling algebra references. He feverishly obliterates his work and launches into a fresh collection.

Within the first few seconds, Danny is at the TAVR, the sleep Laborites, Brunnel College, Binsey, and Wadham. All filmed days apart and miles between the locations, it is clear that Danny's clothes remain the same to provide continuity. Surely, this is an unmistakable tribute to the meticulous planning goes into producing the final product.

The new Lewis series had begun.

However, the filming began at Gaddenston Hall, Hemel Hempstead. The initial scenes were from Trudi's bedroom at the Hall and showed her waking to the sound of a gunshot. With trepidation, she scurries to the bathroom to discover the bloodied body of Tom Polock languishing in the bath. A hooded person is hurriedly fleeing down the immense staircase and out into the shadow of the night. Hauntingly captured flashbacks to the crash scene of Johnny and Danny racing through the gates in a purpose built kit car also add to the collection of the days filming. The dramatic driving scenes necessitate the talents of the full stunt team's presence from the beginning.

The celebratory dinner scene shot is at Gaddenston Hall and as Danny hysterically shrieks at the conglomerate congregation before later avoiding a hasty passionate kiss from Jessica, Paul Herbert plays Danny's double in the stunts. The caterer doubles as a corpse and another caterer doubles as the hoodie, bringing a new meaning to keeping it in the family. All that left apart from the main characters was six dinner guests, two chauffeurs, and four Japanese executives.

Yet, the equipment during this time was up and running by 6.30 a.m. and catering provided for 73 people. The catering was for breakfast, lunch, and sandwiches. The facilities included two make –up trucks, two hobbies, two Single Decker dinning buses, one honey wagon, and a generator. Action cars provided three unit cars, four unit drivers, and two mini buses. An amourer specially called in to oversee the guns.

As the filming continued over the next five days, scenes involving Danny and Rex bitterly arguing over selling the family company were completed. The filming of the external shots with people arriving and leaving persisted whilst the actors acquired clay pigeon shooting expertise, ready for the unwelcome interruption to the day's shooting and business events by Lewis and Hathaway. For continuity, photographs recorded every detail for reference should a repeat shooting be needed. Laboriously documented details such as buttons undone, ties tied remained available for continuity.

The inside scenes are shot showing the home of the Griffon family, where Lewis meets Jess and Tom Pollock the accountant. It is here Lewis discovers Rex's penchant for the odd impotent frolic with Regan. A fact Jess cannot wait to impart to Danny. It is where the discovery that Rex was near the murder scene becomes apparent and Danny's insistent ramblings over his father's premature death, drives his mother to despair.

Once filming at Gaddenston Hall concludes the venue changes to Northwick Park Hospital. A Sunday shoot shows scenes in the mortuary with Lewis and Hathaway. The courtyard of the Lister unit provides the location for Lewis reading Morse's crossword and discovering a ghostly reminder of Danny's previous criminal activities. Apparently, Danny had a youthful enterprise in lethal car modifications. What totally perplexes Lewis is why Morse would be involved with such an inconsequential case. It is also whilst filming at Northwick Park Hospital that the crew capture the scenes of Jessica on the life support machine in High Dependency Unit.

Now into the seventh day of filming the unit moves to a base at Barclay's Bank Sports Ground in Ealing. The script sees a return to Gaddenston Hall as Pollok describes the family history. However, the actual filming for this is at Foxwood Car Park, Ealing. Nearby, still in Ealing, the afternoon scenes of Ivor and his wife returning home conclude the days filming.

The next day moves the crew to The Meridian Estate and Sainsbury's Supermarket, Watford. The Meridian Estate becomes alive as the elated teenagers veer dangerously close to death as a full stunt team provides the dramatic twists and turns for the joyriding.

Sainsbury's provides the location for a theatrically made up, tired Lewis trudging around the supermarket. He meets Dr Jekyll and shares a caffeine-laden coffee before dejectedly returning home to an empty home. These scenes are small unit scenes, filmed later in the evening between nine and ten at night, using a second unit.

The busy itinerary continues with Brunnel University nearby providing parking for the unit. Danny unveils the new Griffon car at the TAVR Centre, Uxbridge and exasperatingly drives off, dramatically screeching to a halt inches away from the top table of a marquee. The scenes of the family duly hosting a tribute to the late Johnny Griffon are already completed.

Close by in Uxbridge is Lewis's House, where he is woken from a jet lagged sleep by the sound of the Hathaway tapping on the window, urging his immediate attention. In reality, Lewis goes from there to film a short sequence at St. Laurence's Church, Cowley, Oxford, at his wife's burial place. He mournfully lays the orchids to rest at his wife's graveside until the urgent tones of Hathaway's mobile phone intrude into Lewis's reminiscences.

Hathaway, Lewis, and some of the team are then in place and ready for the next few days heavy filming in Oxford. Meanwhile, the rest of the cast and crew are gathering in Oxford in preparation for the next locations.

The new Oxford locations are at Magdalen Bridge, The Botanical Gardens, Corpus Christie and St. John's College Boatyard and the path along the river from New Walk to Foley Bridge. With ample parking at Christ Church College for the seventy- three strong crew, the unit swings into action.

The first scenes shot show a decidedly despondent Lewis ponders at the twisting route of the investigation over Magdalen Bridge before Dr Jekyll temptingly offers an ice-lolly and a leisurely summer's stroll in Oxfords striking Botanical Gardens.

As a now familiar Kate refers to Hamlet's Polet unknowingly providing the missing clue to Morse's crossword, Lewis runs off to tell Mrs. Griffon the truth. He hands a bewildered Kate his ice-lolly and hurriedly absconds the scene. A repeated request for Kevin Whately to run faster means shoot after shoot takes place and a demand for fresh ice cream with each new take consequently rises.

Innocuous bystanders agree to become extras, promptly bending over out of his way on command.

The next interruption exasperates the crew as the sound of Magdalen College Bell again halts shooting. Continuity interrupted, the interlude allows the public enjoying the gardens to move past the filming and continue their days outing.

What seems a quiet, leisurely seasonal stroll through the scenic gardens is in fact quite an action-packed event!

Hathaway's expertise in sculling begins to explain the puzzle of Danny's death at Christchurch's and St John's College Boathouse. Lewis and Hathaway play out the scenes only to have to return and redo the whole shoot, as the lighting was unsuitable. The loads of lighting and electrical equipment again snake their way down the narrow paths barely reaching the waters edge.

Small overloaded trailers meander alongside the water's edge, recreating everything to perfection. Photographs align the before and after, as the required scenes are reconstructed. Dejected actors rested until reenacting the whole morning's sequence.

It is also here that Jessica forlornly walks along from New Walk to Foley Bridge, intently gathering stones. The disbelief and grief over her beloved Danny's death keenly etched over her features. Despondently, she becomes absorbed in concentrating on her own demise. Wretchedly walking away from the direction of Binsey, she continues along the gloomy water's edge and gradually fades out of sight.

The scenes rapidly change as Danny is again scrawling frantically across the whiteboard as Lewis and Hathaway pass Colin Dexter as the wag man and enter Wadham College.

The full team has swung in a hive of activity at Wadham College in preparation for their visit. Cars and trucks scatter the horizons down the crowded Catte Street. Lorries speedily unload their wares of lighting, cables, cameras, and tracks.

Everyone labours under his or her familiar roles until the chaotic upheaval begins to take shape and works like a well-oiled machine intent on producing the final masterpiece. With eighty-five people on set, the logistics take some careful planning!

Actors arrive and with well-rehearsed lines, the plot unfolds. Seemingly, with few people in the scene, behind the camera view is a multitude of co-coordinated crewmembers intent on perfection as the cameras roll. Passersby stop for a short while, watching the familiar Oxford scenario, not seen for a while, but not forgotten.

Cars used to ferry the actors around, become part of the plot when visiting Wadham College and tracks lay following the actors every movement, a total of three days filming.

Day 15 and the main unit return to Wadham College and Oriel Square, whilst the second unit provides the shots of the dreamy spires of Oxford and gap filling continuity needs. The first unit films the e-mailing that Danny reverently indulges in and visit with Jess at Oriel Square, Oxford, as she enters for the Endeavour award. It is a moment that genuinely brings a tear to Lewis's eye.

In the next days events, Lewis and Hathaway are off for a days shooting at The Trout, Wolvercote, Oxford.

Preparation for the days shooting began early in the morning as the props arrived. The cold rain blew in the morning breeze as the waft of freshly made coffee permeated through the air, greeting the assembling swarm of crew.

Again, the well-organized crew sprung into frenzied action as health and safety matters saw the wooden bridge swept of wet leaves and carefully primed. Several checks ensured agreement on lighting and areas were meticulously cleared and prepared.

Rowers emerged alongside on the river and people of all ages and gender dawdled into view prepared for the long wait to appear fleetingly as extras.

The saturated area crowded with technicians, camera operator and lighting equipment heaves as solid coils of cables crisscross across the scene. Honey wagons, chuck wagons and all manner of transport painstakingly parked far from the cameras view, the circus had indeed arrived. Seating and umbrellas appeared as props and accommodated the waiting extras.

One solicitous person gainfully employed in wiping the rain off the seating, umbrellas, and tables. The landlord precariously retrieved an old milk carton from the weir and so the scene unfurled.

A deluge of cars become visible following in the footsteps of the lorries through winding, narrow streets and arriving spilling out more familiar faces into the frantic, tumultuous bustle heralding a further burst of noise, clamor and expectancy before the hush descended as the camera began to roll.

As the acting began, repeatedly scenes shot from all angles imaginable mounted into a reel of activity all being transmitted to the post -production team. Even with all the preparation one of the rowers kept capsizing and the shoot waiting for retakes added to the strenuous commotion.

Then as the cameras reeled, the optimistic producer Chris Burt looked on as the assistants weaved and wound their way through takes, vigilantly reviewing the editing to demand more shots or call a close.

The continuity, and director of photography recording each angle, movement, and word, until all were ultimately satisfied and slowly the team preparing for the next part moved on to Binsey, Oxford. Later the location changes to Binsey where the expanse allows parking and the isolation provides a good location for the sound of gunshots. The river scenes are accessible as the land slopes towards the rivers edge.

Danny is first filmed sculling feverishly on the Thames- or at least his double- with divers and safety boats alongside. He also appears practicing firing guns in the woods at Binsey. Jessica, who had begun her journey traveling in the wrong direction to end up at Binsey, reappears.

Vacantly expressionless she wades deeper and deeper into the river, the weight of her pre packed rucksack pulling her down as she disappears into the bottomless muddy depths of the Isis, a shadowy Godstow Abbey behind. An observant angler notices her demise and swiftly fishes her out, the incredulity and sincerity of the scene obviously upsetting.

It is also at Binsey, Oxfordshire that a lone horse rider incorrectly dismounts and discovers Danny Griffon's body believed to be a fatal casualty of the days sculling. Innocent and Lewis seemingly have plenty to discuss at the riverside location, although not necessarily in accord with each other's viewpoint.

The first unit then returns to Wadham College to conclude filming, as Danny's uncle visits the college.
Again, although only a short part appears on television, the flurry of activity again visits Wadham College.

This completed, the units then move to Heathrow as the opportune arrival of Inspector Lewis at Heathrow sees Hathaway displaying his transport home. A quick reminder is issued to all to actors and crew to bring passports, enabling filming both sides of passport control.

Lewis gratefully receives the forgotten orchids as he leaves the airport. He swiftly sprints out of the path of the upsetting jaguar speeding past. This scene provides Lewis of unwelcome memories of changing times. Using a male and female stunt driver, this certainly jolts the viewer who recognizes the significance. With time passing, the location swiftly moves to Slough Station as the location for joy riders breaking into a car.

St Aldates is in the Old DHS Office, Ealing, also the inside of the sleep laborites, the keypads, and Jessica playing. Brunnel University provides other scenes at the sleep laborites.

On day 22, the scenes revert to a mortuary. Danny's body is at St. Peter's Hospital, Chertsey, filming then returns to the sleep laboratory.

The final days filming mean further induced memories rebounding on the journey home past St Giles, the Randolph Hotel and then as if in a time warp, back past the Sheldonian and All Souls. Lewis ultimately ends at his wife's burial place. Moving into the modern era Lewis is on hand to attend a shooting that requires attention a breathalyzed police officer is unable to provide.

The intermission reunites Lewis with old forensic friends, new over -suits and the state of the art soundproofing techniques. Time has indeed moved on and so the filming moves onto postproduction.

Finally, with the whole product treated in postproduction the advertising from pub signs disappear. Conclusively, with eleven million people watching, so begins another era.

Presently, filming is in production for a new series. Involving three episodes, the titles are 'Whom the Gods Would Destroy', 'Old School Ties' and 'Expiation'. Exeter and Christ Church colleges have already hosted the team, as has Broad Street, The Mal Maison Hotel, and the Oxford Student Union. These episodes are for screening in 2007

Production Office
Room 978, The David Lean Building, Shepperton Studios, Studios Road. Middlesex. TW17 0QD.

MOBILE CONTACTS:

Chris White (Loc Manager)	Alex Mercer (2nd AD)	Alan Pinniger (Loc Manager) --
Monique Mussell (Prod Co-ordinator) –		Emma Peter (3rd AD) --

Executive Producers:	Michele Buck	**Date: Friday 5th August 2005**
	Damien Timmer	
	Ted Childs	
Producer/	Chris Burt	**UNIT CALL: 08.00**
2nd Unit Director:		
Co-Producer:	Kate McKerrell	**Breakfast: 07.00**
Director:	Bill Anderson	**Wrap: 19.00**
Line Producer:	Graeme MacArthur	

Sunrise: 05.39   Sunset: 20.58

LOCATION 1:	The Trout Public House, Godstow Road, Wolvercote, Oxford. OX2
LOCATION 2:	The River Isis, Binsey Lane, Binsey, Oxford. OX2
UNIT BASE 1:	Wolvercote Bathing Place Car Park, Wolvercote, Oxford, OX2
UNIT BASE 2:	Old Farm Yard, Binsey Lane, Binsey.
Weather	°C

Sc.	Set.	D/N	Pg.'s	Characters
LOCATION 1				
155	EXT THE TROUT	D4	7/8	1-Lewis, 2-Hathaway
	Lewis and Hathaway go for a beer			
LOCATION 2				
5	EXT ISIS AT BINSEY	D1	1/8	
	The scull is moored, a gunshot is heard			
6	EXT BINSEY WOODED AREA	D1	2/8	3-Danny
	Danny shoots at beer bottles			
119	EXT GODSTOW ABBEY NEAR BOAT YARD	D3	1/8	7-Jessica
	Jessica walks with a heavy rucksack			
120	EXT DANNY'S DEATH SITE	D3	1/8	7-Jessica
	Jessica passes the lock & an angler			
123	EXT DANNY'S DEATH SITE	D3	3/8	7-Jessica
Stunt	*Jessica steps into the water*			
3	EXT ISIS AT BINSEY	D1	2/8	3-Danny
	Danny rows steadily			
	Total Page Count:	**2**	**1/8**	**Pages**

No.	ARTIST	CHARACTER	P/UP	D/R		M/UP&HAIR	COS	Travel	On Set
1	Kevin Whately	DI Lewis	07.05	Hobby # 1	No	07.30	07.55	08.00
2	Laurence Fox	DS Hathaway	07.20	Hobby # 2	Nil	07.45	07.55	08.00
3	Charlie Cox	Danny Griffon	10.00	3-Way # 1	Nil	10.45	10.30	-	11.00
7	Flora Spencer Longhurst	Jessica Pollock	12.00	3-Way # 2	Nil	12.30	12.15	-	14.00

Stand-ins:

David Adams	Lewis / Utility	-	-	-	-	-	08.00

Background Artists:

CHARACTERS	SCENES	NAMES	D/R	M-UP	COST	On Set
Pub Drinkers/Passers	155	Sue Hallet, Abi Wedmore, Anne Morgan, Angela Tizley, Pauline Richardson, John Richardson,	3-Way # 3	07.45	07.30	08.00
Angler	120, 123	Alvin Roy	3-Way # 3	10.45	10.30	11.00

Requirements:

ART DEPT/PROPS:	As per Robin Tarsnane	and Colin Thurston	to inc:
BOATS:	Sculling advisor Jim Ronaldson	to provide 1 x Scull, 1 x 17' Camera Punt. Safety Diver Chris White (t to	
	provide Safety Boat all called to location 2 for 10.30		
STUNTS:	As per Stunt Coordinator Dave Foreman	to inc: called to location 2 for 13.00	
ARMOURER:	As per Bapty's - Faujja Singh	to inc; Danny's Gun called to location 2 for 10.30	
CAMERA:	As per Chris O'Dell	inc: 2nd Camera; Additional Loader Francesco Ferrari	
GRIPS:	As per Warwick Drucker	to inc:	
MEDICAL:	Unit Paramedic Gavin Hewson	c/o A+E Medical Support	

Also used in Filming

The Botanic Gardens are also in Midsommer Murders (1997).
Gaddeston Place appearing in Little Britain (2003), Foyle's War (2002), Jeeves and Wooster (1990), Lady Chatterley (1993) and Jonathon Creek (2001) amongst many others.

The Hemel Hempstead area is the setting for Stardust 1997.

Northwick Park Hospital is a location for The Omen (1976), Fawlty Towers (1975) and Green Wing (2004).

Trivia

The Dead of Jericho

Colin Dexter's appearance Man passing Morse when visiting Ned
Murdock at Magdalene College

No of Drinks for Morse   **No of Drinks for Lewis**
6 Pts of Beer   2 Pts Beer
1 Cup of Tea
Pathologist- Max
Body Count
Anne Staveley, George Jackson

The Silent World of Nicholas Quinn

Colin Dexter's appearance Man Drinking in the Syndicate in Opening
Credits

No of Drinks for Morse   **No of Drinks for Lewis**

1 Glass Sherry   1 Cup of Tea
4 Whiskeys   1 Glass Sherry
One Gin & Tonic   two Pts Beer
Two Pts Beer

Pathologist- Max
Body Count
Nicholas Quinn, Philip Ogleby

Service of All the Dead

Colin Dexter's appearance Man standing with woman with bike when Morse goes to see Archdeacon

Maureen Bennett Played a part of a wife in this episode she was later to appear in Greeks Bearing Gifts as Val Lewis Robbie Lewis's wife.

No of Drinks for Morse

1 Glass Sherry
2 Pts Beer

No of Drinks for Lewis

1 Glass Sherry
2 Pts Beer

Pathologist- Max

Body Count
Lionel Pawlen, Simon Pawlen, Peter Morris, Paul Morris, Brenda Josephs, Harry Josephs

The Wolvercote Tongue

Colin Dexter's appearance Man behind Morse in the Chapters Bar of the Randolph Hotel

No of Drinks for Morse

3 Pts of Beer
1 Gin & Tonic

No of Drinks for Lewis

2 Pts Beer
1 Cup of Tea

Pathologist- Max

Body Count
Dr. Theodore Kemp, Marion Kemp, Laura Poindexter, Lucy Downes

Last Seen Wearing

Colin Dexter's appearance Man walking across quad when Morse visits Sheila Phillipson in library

No of Drinks for Morse
Two Glass of wine
4 Pts of Beer
1 Glass Whiskey
1 Cup of Tea
1 Cup of Coffee

No of Drinks for Lewis
one Glass of Wine
2 Cups of Coffee
½ Pint Beer

Pathologist- Max

Body Count
Cheryl Baines

The Settling of the Sun

Colin Dexter's appearance Doctor sitting on next bed to Jane in final scene

No of Drinks for Morse
2 Pts Beer
1 Glass White Wine
1 Cup of Tea

No of Drinks for Lewis
1 Pt Beer

Body Count
Graham Daniel, Kurt Friedman, aka Michael Robson
 Yukio Li, Reverend Robson, Yukio Li (Decoy)

Last Bus to Woodstock

Colin Dexter's appearance Man behind Morse in Crowther's lecture

No of Drinks for Morse	No of Drinks for Lewis
Two Glass Whiskey	2 Orange juices
1 Cup of Tea	1 Cup of Tea
2 Pts of Beer	1 Pt of Beer
1 Cup of Tea	

Pathologist- Max

Body Count

Sylvia Kane

Ghost in the Machine

Colin Dexter's appearance Man sitting near the Master in the opening scene (

No of Drinks for Morse	No of Drinks for Lewis

Pathologist- Dr. Grayling Russell

Body Count
Roger Meadows, Sir Julius Hanbury

The Last Enemy

Colin Dexter's appearance Man walking along canal bank in opening scene

No of Drinks for Morse
4 Glasses Whiskeys
4 Coffees
One Pt of Beer
One Glass Wine

No of Drinks for Lewis
3 Coffees
1 unknown drink

Pathologist- Dr. Grayling Russell

Body Count
Nicholas Ballarrat, Sir Alexander Reece, Dr. David Kerridge

Deceived by Flight

Colin Dexter's appearance Man Walking behind Lewis and Roland in College

No of Drinks for Morse
3 Cups of Tea
2 Pts of Beer
2 Cups of Coffee
1 Glass White Wine
Irish coffee

No of Drinks for Lewis
1 Orange Juice
1 Cup of Coffee
1 Cup of Tea

Pathologist- Dr. Grayling Russell

Body Count

Anthony Don, Peter Foster
2 Bodies found in a Shop (Arson)

The Secret of Bay 5B

No of Drinks for Morse
4 Pts of Beer
3 Glasses Of Whiskey

No of Drinks for Lewis
1 Glass of Water
1 Orange Juice

Body Count
George Henderson, Brian Pierce, Michael Gifford

Pathologist- Dr. Grayling Russell

The Infernal Serpent

Colin Dexter's appearance Man in chapel at funeral

No of Drinks for Morse
2 Pts of Beer
Juice
Pathologist None

No of Drinks for Lewis
2 Glasses of Orange

Body Count
Matthew Copley-Barnes, Mrs. McGovern, Dr. Julian Dear

The Sins of the Fathers

No of Drinks for Morse
1 Cup Black Coffee
1 Pt of Beer
I Glass of Whiskey

No of Drinks for Lewis
1 Cup of Coffee
½ Pt of Beer
1 Bottle of Beer

Pathologist- Dr. Halliday

Body Count
Trevor Radford
Stephen Radford
Alfred Nelson

Driven to Distraction

Colin Dexter's appearance Man in launderette with Tim Ablett and
Angie Howe

No of Drinks for Morse
2 Cups of Coffee
Three Bottles of Beer
1Pt of Beer
1 Cup of Coffee
1 Cup of Tea

No of Drinks for Lewis
2 Cups of Coffee

Body Count
Jackie Thorn, Paula Steadman, Derek Whittaker

Masonic Mysteries

Colin Dexter's appearance Man in choir next to Morse

No of Drinks for Morse	No of Drinks for Lewis
½ Tin of Beer	2 Cups of Coffee
4 ½ Pts of Beer	1 Pt of Beer

Body Count
Hugo De Vries, Desmond McNutt, Beryl Newsom

Second Time Around

Colin Dexter's appearance Man at Trout Inn when Morse meets Barbara Redpath

No of Drinks for Morse	No of Drinks for Lewis
1 Glass of Brandy	3 Cups of Coffee
1 Glass White Wine	1 Glass Wine
1 Glass Orange Juice	
Two Pts of Beer	

Body Count
Charlie Hillian, John Mitchell

Fat Chance

Colin Dexter's appearance Man in college grounds when Hilary
Dobson goes in for interview

No of Drinks for Morse
1 Glass of Orange Juice
One Pt Beer
1 Cup of Tea
1 Cup of Coffee
1 Glass White Wine

No of Drinks for Lewis
1 Glass of Orange Juice

Body Count
Victoria Hazlett

Who Killed Harry Field

Colin Dexter's appearance Man in-group when Ian Matthews presents
Morse with postcard

No of Drinks for Morse
1 Glass White Wine
Juice
Three Pts Beer
Five Whiskeys
Body Count
Harry Field, Paul Eirl

No of Drinks for Lewis
2 Glasses of Orange

Greeks Bearing Gifts

Colin Dexter's appearance Man in college porter's lodge when Morse leaves after dinner with Jerome Hogg

No of Drinks for Morse
3 Cups of Coffees
2 Glasses White Wine
One Glass of Whiskey

No of Drinks for Lewis
None

Body Count
Nicos Capparis
Friday Rees
Maria Capparis

Promised Land, (aka Inspector Morse in Australia)

No of Drinks for Morse
1 Glass of Orange Juice
1 Glass White Wine
1 Cup of Coffee

No of Drinks for Lewis
4 Pts of Beer
1 Cup of Coffee
1 Cup of Tea

Body Count
Paul Matthews, Mike Harding, Ann's Mum, 2 Policemen in shoot out, Sergeant Scott Humphries.

Dead on Time

Colin Dexter's appearance Man at Reception after Schubert Concert

No of Drinks for Morse
One Glass of Champagne
1 Glass of Lemonade
One Pt of Beer
1 Cup of Tea

No of Drinks for Lewis
1 Pt of Beer
1 Cup of Tea

Body Count
Henry Fallon, Susan Fallon

Happy Families

Colin Dexter's appearance Tramp Drinking from Bottle near Mitre Pub

No of Drinks for Morse
1 Cup of Coffee
One Glass of Red Wine

No of Drinks for Lewis
No Drinks

Body Count
Sir John Balcombe, Harry Balcombe, James Balcombe,
Steven Ford, Lady Emily Balcombe

The Death of the Self

Colin Dexter's appearance Man three seats to Morse's left in closing opera scene
John Thaw's wife Shelia Hancock made an (uncredited) appearance in this episode

No of Drinks for Morse

1 Glass of Water
1 Glass White Wine
1 Glass Red Wine
I Cup of Coffee
Cappuccino

No of Drinks for Lewis

2 Glasses of Water
2 Glasses of Beer

Body Count
May Lawrence, Judith Haines

The Only Episode that did not Feature the Mk 2 Jag

Absolute Conviction

Colin Dexter's appearance Man in prison church when Brian Thornton preaches

No of Drinks for Morse

2 Pts of Beer
3 Cups of Coffee
1 Cup of Tea

No of Drinks for Lewis

1 Pt of Beer
1 Cup of Tea

Body Count
Lawrence Cryer, Roland Sherman aka Harold Manners

Cherubim and Seraphim

Colin Dexter's appearance Man next to Dr. Collier at presentation

No of Drinks for Morse
2 Pts of Beer
2 Cups of Coffee

No of Drinks for Lewis
1 Cup of Tea
1 Glass of Orange Juice
1 Cup of Coffee

Body Count
Jacko Lever, Dr. Desmond Collier, Marilyn Garrett

Deadly Slumber

Colin Dexter's appearance College porter showing Morse and Lewis to John Brewster

No of Drinks for Morse
1 Glass Whiskey
One Pt of Beer
One Glass of White Wine
2 Cups of Coffee

No of Drinks for Lewis
no drinks

Body Count
Dr. Matthew Brewster, Dr. Claire Brewster, Michael Steppings, Avril Steppings

The Day of the Devil

No of Drinks for Morse
One Glass of Whiskey

No of Drinks for Lewis

Body Count
John Peter Barrie, Steven Trevors

Twilight of the Gods

Colin Dexter's appearance Man in Sheldonian Theatre behind Lord
Hinksey

No of Drinks for Morse
No Drinks

No of Drinks for Lewis
No Drinks

Body Count
Neville Grimshaw

Specials

The Way through the Woods

Colin Dexter's appearance Man at concert with Morse in opening scene

No of Drinks for Morse
2 Cups of Tea
2 Pts of Beer
Juice
1 Glass Red Wine
1 Cup of Coffee

No of Drinks for Lewis
1 Cup of Tea
2 Glasses of Orange

Pathologist -Dr. Laura Hobson

Body Count
Steven Parnell, George Daley, Cathy Michaels,
David Michaels, James Myton

Pathologist -Dr. Laura Hobson

The Daughters of Cain

Colin Dexter's appearance Mr. Humphreys - Man with Crutches in
Hospital Waiting Room

No of Drinks for Morse
2 Glasses of Whiskey
3 Pts of Beer
1 Cup of Coffee
1 Cup of Tea
Pathologist -Dr. Laura Hobson

No of Drinks for Lewis
2 Pts of Beer
1 Cup of Tea
one Glass of Pimms
1 Cup of Coffee

Body Count
Ted Brooks, Julia Stevens, Dr. Felix McClure

Death Is Now My Neighbour

Colin Dexter's appearance Vicar saying grace at college dinner

No of Drinks for Morse

2 Cups of Coffee

Juice

Two Pts of Beer

One Glass of Whiskey

One Glass of Brandy

Pathologist -Dr. Laura Hobson

No of Drinks for Lewis

two Glasses of Orange

Body Count

Rachel James, Geoffrey Owens, Shelly Cornford

The Wench Is Dead

Colin Dexter's appearance Man at conference in opening scene

No of Drinks for Morse Kershaw

Sip of Water

1 Cup of Coffee

Two Pts Beer

One Glass of Orange Juice

The Wench Is Dead is the only episode that Kevin Whately (D.S.Lewis) did not appear in.

No of Drinks for

1 Cup of Coffee

½ Pt of Beer

Pathologist -Dr. Laura Hobson

Body Count

Alfred Musson, Rory Jack Oldfield

Unknown Peasant Girl

The Remorseful Day

Colin Dexter's appearance Man in Wheelchair in Saga Group at Magdalen Bridge

No of Drinks for Morse
Water with Alka Seltzer Juice
Two Glasses of Water
One Pt of Beer
Three Glasses of Whiskey
Final Drink I/V Drip
Pathologist -Dr. Laura Hobson

No of Drinks for Lewis
2 Glasses of Orange

Ailish Hurley was the bar manager of Chapter's Bar (now the Morse Bar), Randolph Hotel, Oxford. As a good friend of Colin Dexter, she was a continual source of inspiration to him, persuading him to carry on writing the Inspector Morse novels. As a mark of respect, he requested a cameo role for her in the final Inspector Morse film, "The Remorseful Day", where she is briefly seen serving coffee to Morse and Sandra Harrison. Sadly, she died of cancer on 25 September 2005

Body Count
Yvonne Harrison, Harry Repp, Paddy Flynn
John Barron, Chief Insp. Endeavour Morse

Police Stations

Wellington Place, High Street, Harefield, Hertfordshire – series 6, 7 & 8.
Finchley T.A Centre – The Remorseful Day.
Southall, Middlesex – series 1 & 2.
Plus, studio locations.

Lewis

Colin Dexter's appearance College porter pointing out Danny's room when Lewis and Hathway go to interview him

No of Drinks for Lewis

2 Cups of Coffee

No Drinks for Hathaway

1 Cup of Coffee

Pathologist -Dr. Laura Hobson

Body Count
Regan Peveril, Ivor Denniston, Annie Denniston (uncredited)
Danny Griffon

In Conclusion

As Margaret Kemp, one resident of Brookside, Weston Turville, Buckinghamshire expresses-

"Having such a prestigious series as Morse filmed in our street, and meeting and talking to the actors, is very exciting, adding more than a little colour to everyday life"

This is also true in referring to the journey of writing this book. With great admiration of the writing, acting, and dedication of all those involved in the Inspector Morse Series, it was fascinating to explore a little further. The opportunity to meet and talk to others with an appreciation of the series meant meeting people from recognizable celebrities to people with a wealth different life experiences. It has meant speaking to writers who were driving down the freeway in California, sheep farmers in Australia, members of the Town and Gown that is Oxford, those watching crop circles in Wiltshire to those in their own homes. It has meant traveling to wonderful locations throughout Britain, from the opulence and grandeur of the Morse Bar at the Randolph Hotel, to the isolated tip of North Wales.

From the cast and crew together with the people whose homes, pubs, churches appeared, there has been one common denominator. A love of Morse and eagerness to share experiences, combined with warmth of character towards others with a similar appreciation. Such warmth positively illustrates the affection of Inspector Morse throughout generations, classes, continents, race, gender, and vocations. There are no boundaries to the appeal of Inspector Morse.

It is hoped that the essence of those feelings have been portrayed in the writing of this book.

And finally ... the authors, Paul & Jan Allen got married on 18th October 2006 at The Dexter Rooms Registrars Office, Oxford. Their reception was at The Randolph Hotel, Oxford and their honeymoon began at The Ship Inn, Aberdaron, North Wales. Not many people can say location managers for Inspector Morse originally found their locations for a wedding!

ACKNOWLEGDEMENTS

Terry Ackland- Snow (production designer), Graham Apthorpe (Cowra NSW.Government Australia.), Auberge du Lac, Alison(Bray Church Choir), Harry Barnes (Dialogue Editor), Maggie Bradley (introduction to Bray Church),Sarah Bird (Casting Director), Ian Berg (New Jag Owner,) BBC Radio Berks Listeners, BBC Radio Oxford Listeners, Bray Church, Blenhiem Palace, Borehamwood & Elstree Times, Bray Bell Ringers, John the Bookman, Bristol Television and Film Services, Tom Brown, Brownie (Grips), Peter Buckman (Writer), Graham Bucknell, Canowindra Cabonne Shire Council, Chris Dunn (Library Manager Radlett Library), Chris Burt (Producer Morse & Lewis), Chief Guide for the Friends Kensal Green Cemetery,), Tim Coghlan and Richard Hill (for use of the article in the Wench is Dead). Josef Dbache (Post-Production), Robert Noel, College of Arms (London), Fliss Coombs (Publicist), Vicky de Lacy (Australian Nurse), Didcot Railway Centre (Jeanette Howse), Dorney Court, Ewan.(West London Film Office), Sheila Ferguson (Press Office Ashford and St Peter's Hospitals NHS Trust), Suzanne Fleetwood, Rosslyn Finn (Australia), Steve Fish (Sound), Derek Fowles, Kate Gardner (Front of House Manager Pitt Rivers Museum),Glynn (From Exeter College Oxford), Greyhound Pub (Aldbury Herts), Guy From (St Andrew's Bookshop St Albans, Herts).Pauline Harlow (Script Supervisor) Mark Hellings, Carol Hodson (Jaguar UK), Jericho Echo, Lawrence Fox, Kevin Whately and Colin Dexter (photographs) Margaret Kemp, Tony Lewery (Barge Painter), Alan Lister, (From. Brakespears Henley), Lynn and Mick Maloney, Maureen (From Pearce Coaches Oxford), Jill and Ken McDonald, David McHenry, Theresa Healey,(Brisbane, Australia), Members from the Joe's John Thaw website www.johnthaw.topcities.com Media & Communications Unit (Oxford Hospitals), Emma Middleton Black Country Living Museum, Julian Mitchell (Writer), Robin Nye (New College Oxford),Barrington Pheloung (Composer),Adrian and June Potts(Barge Inn Honey Street Wiltshire), Jaynie Sandall, (proof reading) Pitts Rivers (John Simmons Head of Technical Services), Alan Pinniger (Location Manager), The Reverend George Repath Vicar of St. Michael's Bray with Braywood, Mr. & Mrs. Redmond, Roger (From David A C Royle & Co Ltd), Ann Runeckles (Studio Liaison The Pinewood Studios Group),

Ray Payne and the Regulars, Fox & Castle Pub Old Windsor, James Scott (Writer),Wales Screen Commission, Roz Smith, Andrew Speller (Camera Operator), Bob Sperling, Matthew Stephenson (Global Retreat Centre Nuneham Courtney), Amanda Street (Director DNA Music Ltd), Mrs. P.A. St Clair (Oxford Resident) John Styles (Punch and Judy Man), Robin Tarsnane(Production Designer), Colin Thurston (Props Master), Clive Tickner, Jackie Toomey (St Albans Museums), Frank & Jackie.Tofield (My Lady Wedding Cars), Trout Pub (Godstow Oxford), Mrs. Satu Vartiainen, Henry Vivian-Neal, Timothy Walker (Director University of Oxford Botanic Garden & Harcourt Arboretum), Paul Weston, Chris White (Location Manager), Villagers of Wytham, Oxford, Ben Wilson (Marketing Department Andrews Estates Agents), Wim (Thornton's Bookshop) and with thanks to everyone else that helped in compilation of this book.

Also with thanks for the offer to contribute after the filming of Harry Potter is completed – Cliff Lanning and Russell Lodge. Hopefully to be added in the next addition.

Printed in the United Kingdom
by Lightning Source UK Ltd.
119053UK00001B/68

9 781846 855115